Our
Canada
Picture Perfect

Our Canada

Picture Perfect

BOOK PROJECT STAFF

Editor: Pamela Johnson

Senior Designer: Andrée Payette

Assistant Designer: Ann Devoe

Contributing Editors: Jesse Corbeil and Robert Ronald

Copy Editor and Proofreader: Robert Ronald

Photo Editor: Rachel Irwin

Production Coordinator: Gillian Sylvain

Production Manager: Gordon Howlett

OUR CANADA MAGAZINE CONTRIBUTING STAFF

Production Editor: Simon McDermott

Assistant Art Director: Robert Bigras

Writers and Editors: Gary George and Maryanne Gallagher

READER'S DIGEST ASSOCIATION (CANADA) ULC

President and CEO
Antonio Cioffi

Vice-President, Editorial
Robert Goyette

Manager, English Book Editorial
Pamela Johnson

THE READER'S DIGEST ASSOCIATION, INC.

President and Chief Executive Officer
Mary G. Berner

President, Canada and Latin America
Patricia Hespanha

OUR CANADA, PICTURE PERFECT

An original book first published in 2010 by *Our Canada*,
an imprint of the Reader's Digest Association (Canada), ULC
© 2010 by Reader's Digest Association (Canada) ULC
© 2010 by The Reader's Digest Association, Inc.
© 2010 by Reader's Digest Association Far East Ltd.
Philippine Copyright 2010 by The Reader's Digest Association
  Far East Ltd.

Library and Archives Canada Cataloguing in Publication

Our Canada picture perfect / the editors of Our Canada.

ISBN 978-1-55475-034-4

   1. Canada--Pictorial works. 2. Canada. FC59.O97 2009
971.07022'2   C2009-906475-8

Note: All original contributor names and addresses were correct at the time of
publication in *Our Canada* Magazine. The editors have taken reasonable
measures to confirm the accuracy and correct attribution of the quotations in
this book. Information that will enable the publisher to rectify
errors or to include proper credit in future printings will be welcome.

We are committed to both the quality of our products and the service
we provide to our customers. If you have any comments about
the content of this book, please write to:
The Book Editor, Reader's Digest Association (Canada) ULC,
1100 René-Lévesque Blvd. W., Montreal, QC H3B 5H5

For more Our Canada products and information, visit our website at
www.ourcanada.ca

  and

For more Reader's Digest products and information, visit our website at
www.readersdigest.ca

Printed in China
10 11 12 13 / 4 3 2 1

This book is dedicated to Canadians everywhere.
If our landscapes—the rivers, hills and valleys,
rugged coasts, mountains and lakes are the
tapestry, then each adult and child is a thread that
helps bind it together. It is your shared love of this
land that is etched across each page and
confirms that our Canada is indeed picture perfect.

Thank you.

Table of Contents

The North

Introduction

Picture Perfect; what a fantastic and fitting title for this wonderful book devoted to a subject so close to all our hearts—Canada. You are about to travel the length and breadth of this great land through the pages of this beautiful book, which has been compiled from some of the wonderful images and stories from the first five years of *Our Canada* magazine.

I have been a part of the *Our Canada* story since the beginning, and over the years I have been fortunate enough to speak to many contributors to the magazine from across this country; and in so doing they have discovered that I am actually not a native Canadian. What? You work at a magazine called *Our Canada*, but you're not from here? Born and raised in England, I only moved to Canada in 1999, in my mid 30s. So many wasted years, for within moments of touching down in Montreal, I'd fallen in love with this city, this belle province, this fantastic country. And with every passing day since, I've continued to fall ever deeper in love with my new home. Many times, in moments of reflection, I have tried to pinpoint what it is that attracts me. Is it the four definite seasons I experience here in Central Canada; the awe-inspiring power of a winter storm in full swing, the scent of spring, humidity of a steamy, lazy August afternoon and the crescendo of colour as fall turns the hills and valleys to reds and golds? Is it the salt air, rocky coastlines and surf-pounded beaches of the Atlantic provinces that call to me on a sea breeze?

Perhaps it's the giant skies and rolling fields of the prairies, the contrast between the mountainous Rockies

and the lush, green forests of Western Canada or the midnight sun, months of darkness, ice, snow and wilds of the North that take my breath away. You know, I think it's all of the above—wrapped in the warmth of the Canadian people—admired the world over—who live in each region that make me realize I have found the home of my dreams, my one true north. No, I wasn't born here, but what a testament to this great land that no matter from where you hail, the colour of your skin, your culture or your creed, all are welcome here.

Our Canada magazine was born of a 2003 *Reader's Digest* photo contest. The response was huge! It was obvious that Canadians across the country were crying out for a magazine for them, by them. So, in January 2004 the first issue of *Our Canada* rode the presses.

Since then, *Our Canada* and now *More of Our Canada* magazines have gone on to weave themselves into the very tapestry of this country. Thousands of Canadians have had their stories and photos published in this country's favourite reader-written magazine. But *Our Canada* has become more than just a place to tell stories and share photos, it has become a meeting place, a growing community that celebrates together all that is good about our home and native land.

This book is far more than a collection of wonderful photos and informative facts about a country, it is a celebration of a land like no other.

Simon McDermott

SIMON MCDERMOTT

The *Our Canada* and *More of Our Canada* team

Just like you, the team that compiles each issue of *Our Canada* is close knit.
A small group of dedicated individuals, they all share a love of this land
and a passion for helping every Canadian's voice be heard.
Meet the team.

"The more tranquil a man becomes, the greater is his success, his influence, his power for good. Calmness of mind is one of the beautiful jewels of wisdom."

—James Allen

Robert Goyette If Robert were to cut himself he would likely bleed ink, for he is a voracious reader and writer. Robert began his career as a reporter at *The Montreal Star* newspaper in the 70s. In 1979 he joined *Sélection du Reader's Digest*, where he worked tirelessly to build local content for Quebec readers. He moved to the magazine *L'Actualité* as managing editor in 1987, before rejoining *Sélection* in 1994. Robert was appointed editor-in-chief in 1999. The following year saw Robert become vice-president of Reader's Digest Magazines Canada Ltd., and the year after that he became chair of the Reader's Digest Foundation of Canada. In addition, he is also responsible for book and web editorial for Reader's Digest Canada. Robert is the proud father of three boys. In his free time (not that he has a lot of it) Robert likes to play golf and, of course, read.

"The road to a friend's house is never long."

—Danish Proverb

Simon McDermott was born and raised in England. After travelling extensively in Europe, the Middle East and the United States, he eventually followed the woman of his dreams (a Canadian, naturally) to these shores in 1999. As fresh starts appeared to be the order of the day, Simon began studying journalism at Montreal's Concordia University and working as a proofreader at Reader's Digest to help pay for his tuition.

When *Our Canada* magazine was born in 2004, Simon was on hand to help out. Simon's spare time is completely consumed by his favourite hobby of engaging in mortal hand-to-mouth combat with his stomach...with varying degrees (and pant sizes) of success and failure over the years.

"It all started in a 5,000-watt radio station in Fresno, California. With just a $50-a-week paycheque and a dream."

—Ted Baxter on "The Mary Tyler Moore Show"

Gary George Born and bred in Montreal, Gary is happily married and the proud father of two children, who are now in their early 20s. A graduate of Concordia University's creative writing program, he landed his first writing job at an ad agency in 1985. By the end of the 1980s, he was hired by *The Gazette* (Montreal's English daily newspaper), where he spent a decade gaining experience in marketing communications, graphic design, print production, radio promotions and editorial. From there, it was on to Reader's Digest Magazines Canada, where he wrote promotional material and direct mail campaigns—mainly in support of the brand new *Our Canada* magazine. When a position become available on *Our Canada*'s editorial team, Gary leapt at the opportunity...and the rest, as they say, is history.

> *"A man travels the world over in search of what he needs and returns home to find it."*
>
> —George Moore

Robert Bigras Born in Montreal, Robert began working as an illustrator after completing a college diploma in visual arts and a B.A. in graphic design at the University of Quebec at Montreal. Among other accomplishments, Robert won first prize in an international poster competition sponsored by UNESCO, and was later selected for a graphic design internship in Paris. He then worked in art direction on the French edition of *Chatelaine* for several years. Associated with Reader's Digest Magazines Canada since 2000, Robert has played a pivotal creative role with *Our Canada* since its inception. When he is away from the office, chances are Robert is indulging in one of his three other passions in life—family time, travel and gourmet food—or, ideally, all three at once.

> *"It is not true that people stop pursuing dreams because they grow old, they grow old because they stop pursuing dreams."*
>
> —Gabriel Garcia Marquez

Tania Dallaire decided at the age of 12 she wanted to be a graphic designer. She had no idea what a graphic designer did but she liked the sound of it. Tania studied Graphic Design at Quebec's Laval University, before moving to Montreal. Recently, she attended a workshop at The International Summer School of Percé, Que., presented by Ian Anderson, founder of The Designers Republic, an avante-garde British design studio. Tania loves to travel and says that working at *Our Canada* allows her to do so a little every day. She also enjoys reading and recently bought a book entitled *1,001 Books You Should Read Before You Die*. Tania truly wishes to read all of the books listed but having read only about 100 so far, she realizes that she has a long way to go.

> *"Success is not final, failure is not fatal: It is the courage to continue that counts."*
>
> —Winston Churchill

Maryanne Gallagher A native Montrealer, Maryanne is happily married and, along with her husband, John, enjoys camping in summer, snowshoeing in winter and rooting for her beloved Montreal Canadiens.

After earning a B.A. in English Literature from McGill University, she began working for Reader's Digest for what was supposed to be a six-month stint—that was 23 years ago.

After holding various positions within the Operations department and taking magazine writing courses at night, she eventually got the opportunity to work part time for *Our Canada*. Shortly after that, a full-time position opened up: Maryanne has now fulfilled her long-held ambition of becoming a full-time editor, and could not be happier about it.

> *"It takes a long time to become young."*
>
> —Pablo Picasso

Jennifer De Freitas Jennifer is a third-year journalism student at Montreal's Concordia University and the newest member of the *Our Canada* family, having joined the team as a part-time writer and editor in July 2009. Jen says working at *Our Canada* is the ultimate experience, as every contributors' story she reads takes her to a beautiful part of Canada she may otherwise have not discovered. When she isn't travelling the country through the pages of *Our Canada*, Jen likes to unwind by reading a fashion magazine or watching a romantic comedy with her family and boyfriend.

BRITISH COLUMBIA

> MY FRIENDS OFTEN ASK ME IF
> I WOULD LIKE TO CLIMB MOUNT
> EVEREST. I ALWAYS RESPOND,
> "WHY TRAVEL THOUSANDS OF
> MILES FROM HOME WHEN WE HAVE
> ALL THIS GRANDEUR RIGHT HERE
> IN OUR OWN BACKYARD."
> —DAVE ROTHWELL

◄ **Rosedale** The Fraser Valley
is an area of great fertility.
Here, the Cascades mountain
range makes a dramatic backdrop for a field in a tulip farm.

British Columbia: So Much to Explore, So Little Time

Dave Rothwell

Growing up in a small town in the Kootenays, I can still remember my amazement as we drove through the Rockies on our yearly pilgrimage to visit family in Calgary. Staring out the back window of the old family sedan as snow capped peaks rose majestically around on all sides. It was not until many years later that I would truly come to realize how those views would shape my very existence.

While attending camp on Kootenay Lake in my early teens I was invited to hike into Kokanee Glacier Provincial Park. This was my first experience into B.C.'s backcountry, and I was absolutely blown away by the alpine meadows, the rugged peaks and the simplicity of living life (if only for a few days) by carrying all that I needed on my back. That was it, I was hooked! That was 30 years ago, and the draw of the mountains and its rugged untamed beauty still pulls my strings just as it did back then.

I live in the Okanagan Valley, which is a year-long playground. Beautiful sunny days can be filled with biking, hiking, waterskiing or just simply lazing on a beach with a good book. Few places in Canada would allow you to go snow skiing in the morning, play a round of golf in the afternoon, then sit out on a patio in the evening at one of the many magnificent wineries enjoying a glass of local vintage while watching a beautiful sunset on the lake.

I can't lay claim to be an expert on all of B.C., but most places I've visited certainly have their own mystical claim. From whale watching off Vancouver Island to the splendour of Victoria's harbour, there is something for every passion. Vancouver's culture, cuisine and nightlife are high on the list, as well as Whistler via the Sea to Sky Highway. If I had to choose one word to describe living in B.C.: "fortunate."

Super-Naturally Beautiful British Columbia

Al Harvey
PHOTOGRAPHER

In addition to the beauty of Canada's westernmost province is the immense diversity of its physical geography. The Rockies run diagonally for almost the entire province, and seem to create a psychological divide from the rest of the nation.

▲ **Spanish Banks** The Spanish Bank beaches, located on Marine Drive in north-western Vancouver, are sectioned into three beaches: East, Extension and West. Low tides here reveal miles of sandy beach, perfect for discovering what the ocean has left behind.

◄ **Vancouver** Nestled between the mountains and the sea, Vancouver is the most populous city in British Columbia, with over half a million residents. Vancouverites enjoy one of the warmest climates in Canada.

Even a native British Columbian like me can't help but be dazzled by landscapes that range from arid to lush rainforest to alpine slopes, and an irregular coastline that features fjords, countless islands and long white sand beaches.

British Columbia is defined by the Pacific Ocean and by the mountains, particularly the Coast Mountains to the west and the Rockies, which run along the Alberta border. The Coast Mountains, outsiders are often surprised to learn, are higher than the Rockies.

In between the two are lesser ranges and the central plateau that forms the watershed of the mighty Fraser River. The forests and mountains in the northern half are endless.

The far northeast borders on the boreal north, while in the far northwest is the Tatshenshini watershed, a pocket of spectacular mountains and valleys, glaciers and grizzlies, rarely seen except by wilderness adventurers.

Along the Pacific coast, freighters, tugboats and fishing boats share the waters with cruise liners, ferries, kayaks and yachts. Seals, otters and various species of whale abound, and the scuba diving here is among the finest in the world for variety, especially in the winter.

Just south of Alaska is Haida Gwaii, the archipelago homeland of the Haida nation. Known as the "Galapagos of the North" for their ecological uniqueness, the southern islands are the promised land for serious sea kayakers. Numerous smaller islands hug a coastline heavily indented with long fjords crowned by glaciers.

Vancouver Island is the largest offshore island. The western terminus of the Trans-Canada Highway at Tofino on its western shore is just north of the immense stretch of white sand at Long Beach, the gateway to Clayoquot Sound, a popular paddling area.

▲ Fraser Valley Mount Baker towers over a Fraser Valley farm. The agricultural and increasingly urban Fraser Valley leads east into the Coast Mountains, beyond which the climate becomes much more arid as the mountains catch most of the ocean's moisture.

▶ Chilcotin River The Chilcotin River, south of Prince George, is considered by many to be among the most challenging spots for whitewater rafting. Also world-renowned for its spectacular scenery, the river winds its way through striking mountains and incredible canyons as it hurries to meet the Fraser River.

On the island's southeastern tip is Victoria, the provincial capital. To the east are the Gulf Islands, a conduit for more than 40 ferries that link the islands with one another and the mainland.

With Victoria and Vancouver and their suburbs, southwestern British Columbia is the most populated. Both cities feature distinct neighbourhoods that reflect the influence of the Europeans and Asians who settled here. Cosmopolitan Vancouver is rich in ethnic restaurants, with something for every palate.

The scenic Sea to Sky Highway takes you to Whistler, a premier ski destination. A hundred kilometres north of Vancouver, Whistler attracts just as many visitors in the summer with its golf courses, bicycle and hiking trails, and chain of small lakes, as well as its proximity to Garibaldi Provincial Park.

Orchards and vineyards dominate the Okanagan Valley, where recreation and easy living abound. In the centre of the valley is Kelowna, a magnet for retirees and tourists, as the Okanagan is blessed with a sunny and dry climate. In fact, the southern end of the valley is home to a small desert near Osoyoos.

To the north of the Okanagan is Shuswap Lake, a sprawling H-shaped body where in the autumn, the famous Adams River sockeye migration occurs. Farther east is the Kootenay Valley, with its wealth of hot springs.

For anyone passionate about the outdoors, British Columbia offers endless opportunities to find remote wilderness adventure.

▲ **Tatlatui Provincial Park** Firewood blooms near Tatlatui Provincial Park in northern British Columbia, east of the Alaskan panhandle. Tatlatui contains many lakes, and is about 240 kilometres north of Smithers on the easterly fringe of the Skeena Mountains. The park is accessible only by float plane, as there is no road access.

◄ **Golden Dreams River** Paddling the gentle current of the River of Golden Dreams near Whistler.

► **Nicola Lake** South of Kamloops is a glacially-formed narrow, deep lake located in the south-central interior of British Columbia. It is home to the Upper Nicola Indian Band.

PACIFIC PLAYGROUND
WATER, WATER, EVERYWHERE...

▲ **Victoria** Fisgard Lighthouse between Esquimalt Harbour and the Strait of Juan de Fuca.

"The sea belongs to whoever sits by the shore."
—Louis Dudek

STRAIT OF GEORGIA
The Strait of Georgia separates the Lower Mainland from the vast expanse of Vancouver Island, and is a marine ecosystem of incredible complexity: it is home to the mighty orca, the otter, the harbour seal, dolphins and seabirds of every description.

HELL'S GATE
The narrowest section of the mighty Fraser River, Hell's Gate, is a rocky gorge only 30 metres across and 180 metres deep.

BURRARD INLET
The Burrard Inlet is a coastal fjord that dates from the last ice age, and separates Vancouver from the North Shore.

▶ **Victoria** The capital's Inner Harbour offers a vibrant street scene, musicians, artists...and a small houseboat community at Fisherman's Wharf.

▲▲ **Wells Gray Provincial Park** The 141-metre Helmcken Falls is Canada's fifth highest waterfall.

▲ **Sunshine Coast** A floating cabin on calm Powell Lake.

◀ **Lake Koocanusa** A young water enthusiast shows off his high-flying moves at a quiet spot on this lake, which was formed by the damming of the Kootenay River in Montana in the mid 1970s.

21

SALMON GLACIER
For a different water experience, look no further than Salmon Glacier, the largest road-accessible icefield in the world. It sits just north of Stewart. The Salmon and nearby Bear Glacier offer a dramatic glimpse at what Canada would have looked like when ice covered the land.

DELLA FALLS
The 440-metre Della Falls is the highest waterfall in Canada, cascading from Della Lake to feed into Drinkwater Creek, and eventually Great Central Lake. The falls are about 60 kilometres from Port Alberni.

PACIFIC RIM NATIONAL PARK
Vancouver Island's Pacific Rim National Park is known for its epic vistas offered by a 10-kilometre strip of sandy coast, washed by Pacific swells, called Long Beach. Although blessed with warm temperatures, its rainfall amounts to more than 300 centimetres annually.

RADIUM HOT SPRINGS POOLS
The Radium Hot Springs pools in Kootenay National Park include the largest in Canada, and at a temperature of about 39°C (103°F), it is a popular destination for spa-lovers. The pools are named for the trace amounts of radon found in the water.

▶ **Okanagan Valley** Spawning kokanee salmon in Kalamalka Lake, near Vernon.

▶▶ **Vancouver Island** Beautiful Brentwood Bay is home to the world-famous Butchart Gardens. It's also a jumping-off point for kayakers, canoeists, sailors and boaters of all kinds.

▼ **French Beach Provincial Park** Southern Vancouver Island offers great whale watching in the spring and fall. It's also a great place to birdwatch, observe bald eagles, otters, seals and sea lions. Or, just take a quiet walk along the shore.

Animals

◄◄ **Golden** A grey wolf picks up speed at the Northern Lights Wildlife Wolf Centre, which opened to the public in 2002.

◄ **Kelowna** A heron searches for a snack in an Okanagan stream.

▼ **Kalamalka Lake Provincial Park** A mountain goat surveys the terrain from the safety of a ledge.

▼▼ **Khutzeymateen Valley** A young grizzly browses in Canada's only dedicated grizzly sanctuary, about 45 km northeast of Prince Rupert.

▲ **Lake Cowichan** Roosevelt elk graze on Vancouver Island.

▶ **108 Mile Ranch** A cougar rests in a tree about 500 km north of Vancouver.

▼ **Gulf Islands** A pair of seals sun themselves on Portland Island.

Views That Take Your Breath Away

Emma Levez Larocque
PHOTOGRAPHER

COASTAL BRITISH COLUMBIA IS SPECTACULAR. FROM THE AIR, ON A SUNLIT DAY, THE MAGIC SEEMS TO STRETCH FOREVER.

My husband, Matt, is a helicopter pilot, and we've lived in Powell River, B.C., for almost ten years now. It's a place of awe-inspiring beauty, and we're fortunate to be able to explore the area from a perspective that most people never get to see. A gateway for outdoor enthusiasts, Powell River is a small, picturesque community nestled on the shore of the Upper Sunshine Coast. When you take to the air in the region, suddenly the world opens up around you. The mountains to the north and east become stepping stones leading to endless valleys, pristine lakes and mountain ranges that make up the backcountry. Heading southeast, you can meander down the Sunshine Coast to Vancouver, passing a collection of charming communities, and watching the magnificent city take shape before you.

What I truly love about flying in a helicopter is the three-dimensional point of view: you see what an eagle sees when it's soaring above land. You can't help but realize how connected we all are to the lands and waters that surround the communities we live in. Coastal British Columbia is as spectacular as any place on earth.

"I feel very lucky to have the opportunity to see the world this way," Matt says. "Many people have no idea what lies just beyond their doorstep—it's something that's hard to imagine if you've never seen it from the air. I like the coast because of the proximity to the ocean, mountains and inlets with long river systems. The mountains in the Powell River area are like a maze; the diversity of their topography is fascinating."

It's true—this is a place where your imagination can really take flight.

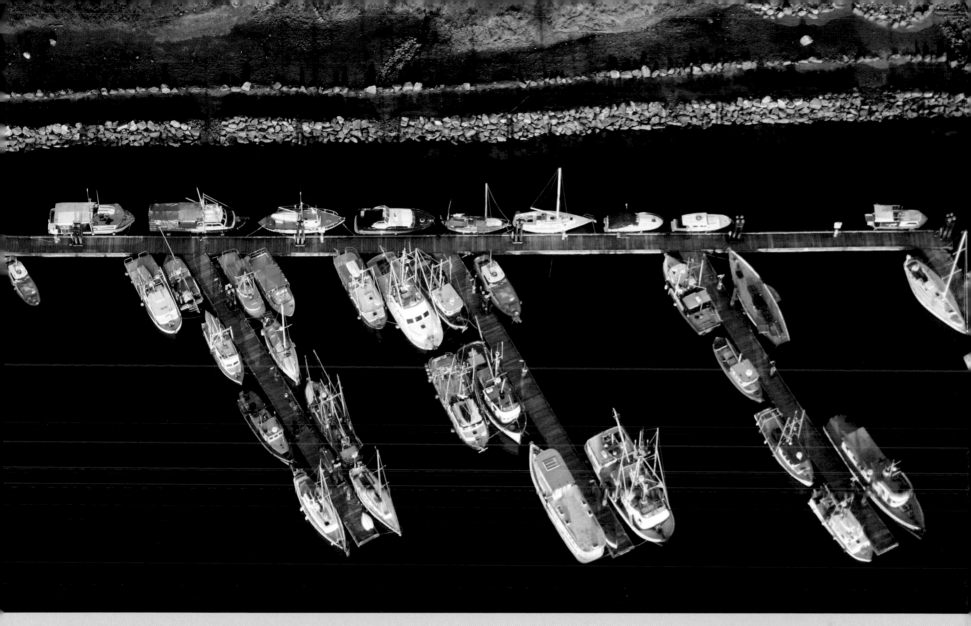

◀ **Vancouver** A cruise ship berthed at Canada Place in the Port of Vancouver, where high-rise towers seem to emerge from the sea.

▲ **Sunshine Coast** Boats in the Westview Harbour, Powell River.

▶ **Sunshine Coast** A ferry sets out from Powell River, headed for Comox on Vancouver Island.

UNIQUE SUPERLATIVES
BRITISH COLUMBIA'S COMMUNITIES

◄ **Kelowna** As the largest urban centre in the Okanagan, Kelowna offers the conveniences of a major city, but still maintains a certain small-town appeal.

"You've probably heard that we can ski within sight of downtown Vancouver and be on the water catching a spring salmon, all in the space of thirty minutes. It's true—as long as your skis have quick-release bindings."
—Denny Boyd

VANCOUVER
In 1886, following the great fire, Vancouver's city hall was a tent. It's come a long way since then. Today's "Hollywood North" is a bustling centre of film and TV production, as well as Canada's busiest seaport. More than two-thirds of recent immigrants arrived from Asian countries, enriching the social mosaic of the city. 2010 saw Vancouver and Whistler welcome the world as hosts of the 21st Winter Olympics.

VICTORIA
Every February, while most of the country is still snowbound, Victoria's Flower Count pits residents against one another to see who can grow the most blooms in his or her garden.

KIMBERLY
At an elevation of 1,113 metres, Kimberley is Canada's highest city and home to "Happy Hans." He is a lifesize, lederhosen-wearing, yodelling, Bavarian figure with a beer mug in his hand, who emerges from the upper story of a steam-driven cuckoo clock, every hour, on the hour.

PRINCE RUPERT
Almost 800 km north of Vancouver, Prince Rupert sits on the north side of Kaien Island, a quick ferry ride from the magical beauty of Haida Gwaii.

BURNABY
Burnaby on the Burrard Peninsula, is the third-largest city in B.C. Its ratio of green space to residents is one of the highest in North America and its close proximity to downtown Vancouver, makes it an extremely attractive place to live. It's also home to world-renowned Simon Fraser University.

KELOWNA
Kelowna is the gateway to the Okagagan Valley and home to legendary creature Ogopogo. His statue can be found near Kelowna's City Park.

TOFINO
Tofino offers nature lovers easy access to the adjacent Clayoquot Sound region and the gorgeous Pacific Rim National Park Reserve.

◄ **Vancouver** A full moon shines over the urban glow of Vancouver, seen from the seawall in Stanley Park.

▶ **Victoria** The Empress Hotel makes a gorgeous backdrop to Victoria's bustling Inner Harbour.

"There was a time in this fair land
when the railroad did not run,
When the wild majestic mountains
stood alone against the sun,
Long before the white man and
long before the wheel,
When the green dark forest
was too silent to be real."

—Gordon Lightfoot

▼ **Mount Revelstoke** two friends enjoy B.C.'s dramatic lanscape from a lookout.

▶ **New Denver** the calm waters of Slocan Lake stretch out beneath a fabulous blue sky.

Okanagan Valley

Gunter Marx
PHOTOGRAPHER

THE OKANAGAN VALLEY, OFTEN CALLED THE FRUIT BASKET OF CANADA, LIES BETWEEN THE CASCADE AND COLUMBIA MOUNTAINS. ITS HEART, OKANAGAN LAKE, AND ITS WARM CLIMATE, MAKE IT ONE OF THE MOST ENTICING SPOTS IN BRITISH COLUMBIA.

▼ **Vaseux Lake** The sheer face of the McIntyre Bluffs overlook this small lake between Oliver and Okanagan Falls.

My wife and travelling companion, Janet, and I enjoy visiting the Okanagan Valley in southern B.C. at every opportunity. It's one of the mildest, driest and most well-irrigated growing climates in Canada—a virtual paradise for fruit cultivation, winemaking and dairy farming, and a popular destination for sightseeing and recreation.

The breathtaking blossom season starts in the semi-arid south Okanagan orchards, in Osoyoos and Oliver, with the appearance of apricot blossoms in early April, followed by peach, pear, plum, cherry and apple blossoms. The blooms continue in the northerly region into mid-May. Prickly pear cactus, with its wonderful yellow flowers, blossoms into late spring. Wildflowers such as the mariposa lily and the black-eyed Susan add to the colourful mix.

▲ **Wine Country** Over the years, many of the region's orchards have been changed over to vineyards for the bustling Okanagan wine industry.

◀ **Kelowna** Though it's not currently in operation, the Okanagan Valley Wine Train used to take wine lovers on a scenic tour through some of the best wine country in Canada.

The Okanagan is truly special at fruit time, especially during the peach harvest in mid-August. Fruit stands and U-pick orchards abound in the south Okanagan, and we inevitably find ourselves on a constant fruit diet. We particularly enjoy buying directly from the farmers. There's no word to describe the flavour of those oversized, just-about-overripe peaches that send juice running down your fingers with every bite.

No place celebrates the peach harvest like Penticton, which hosts the the annual Peach-fest every August, featuring parades, live entertainment and other fun activities.

The Okanagan River Channel in Penticton is also a choice destination for summer-fun enthusiasts who like to float on interlocked rafts and inflatables of all types. As a drive along the main route (Highway 97) through the valley will show you, the Okanagan also offers many other wonderful sandy beaches and lakes for water sports of all kinds.

Another must-see locale is the Pocket Desert, tucked away in the southernmost corner of the valley. This extraordinary habitat is home to an exceptional range of desert animals and plants, some found nowhere else in Canada, and many on the verge of extinction. The shifting sand patterns driven by the wind are a sight to see. For a "close to the land" experience, stop by Osoyoos, where you can try riding into the Pocket Desert on horseback.

▲ **Similkameen Valley** This arid valley was once known for its gold mines, ranching and western heritage. Today, the area is known for its fruit, vegetable and wine production.

◄ **Osoyoos** Spotted Lake is so high in minerals that they form round salt pans in the summer heat.

The First Nations people have a winery in Osoyoos, where you can taste their wine, enjoy a good meal and savour the view of the town and Osoyoos Lake.

If wine tasting is tops on your agenda, you'll want to visit the Okanagan in fall.

The Okanagan is aglow in autumn, as the orchards turn red, and the vineyards turn golden. Sumac bushes are especially colourful dots in the countryside.

The fruit harvest is generally finished by this time, leaving just apples in the central-north Okanagan and pears in the south Okanagan to harvest into October.

Whether it is in winter, spring, summer or fall, B.C.'s very own Garden of Eden is always a joy to visit.

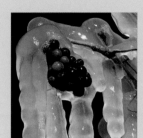

◄ **Ice wine** The Okanagan is becoming well-known for its ice wines.

▼ **Osoyoos** Named for the lake it spans, Osoyoos has been a fur-trade outpost, a cattle town, colonial administrative centre and fruit producer. Today, its wines can hold their own against almost any Californian or French wines.

FOCUS ON VITICULTURE

Wineries of the Okanagan Valley

The exceptional quality of Okanagan wines puts Canada on the vintner's map. The climate and natural landscape provide perfect conditions for cultivating wine grapes. The stunning scenery and over 70 picturesque wineries—some overlooking Okanagan Lake—draw tourists and wine aficionados from around the world.

Okanagan Wine Festivals have been recognized as being among the Top 100 Events in North America and provide a veritable Bacchanalia of wine activities.

The Spring Festival runs through the first weekend in May each year, but the real drawing card to the Okanagan is it's wine-festival season every autumn. For about a two-week period in October, the Okanagan wine-tasting rooms are in full swing, and the region's wineries pair their wines with specially arranged dinners for a set price.

Oliver, the self-proclaimed "Wine Capital of Canada," has its annual Festival of the Grape during this time period. Aside from visiting the many wineries offering their wine for tasting, our favourite activity at this festival is the "grape stomp"—where costumed, barefoot competitors stomp half-barrels full of red grapes, while their harried teammates collect the juice into gallon jugs. The team with the most grape juice is the winner!

The festival atmosphere carries over into winter as well, when the Okaganan's ice wine shares the spotlight with the region's excellent ski hills and resorts, including Big White near Kelowna, Silver Star near Vernon, and Apex near Penticton.

◄ **Merritt** Early morning fishing on Corbett Lake.

▼ **Ferni** The Elk and Bull rivers offer pleasure-seekers a whole range of activities, from a gentle row to the excitement of white-water rafting.

▼▼ **Ganges Harbour** Saltspring Island is the largest of the Gulf Islands. Travel to and from the island is by float plane, boat or ferry.

Boats

◀ **Powell Lake** A floating cabin huddles in the snow. The lake is so deep that it doesn't freeze over in winter.

◀ **Vancouver Island** A fishing boat moored at Port Alice on the Neroutsos Inlet near the north end of Vancouver Island.

▼ **Haida Gwaii** Marinas and harbours welcome boaters at Sandspit and Masset.

WINTER WONDERLANDS
SKIING IS A DANCE AND THE MOUNTAIN ALWAYS LEADS

*"Through the golden glow, on powdered snow
When the moon comes rolling along,
On a homeward trail, you can hear the wail,
of the whole gang singing a song."*

—Stompin' Tom Connors

WINTER WEATHER
Winter has many faces in B.C.: Vancouver Island has some of the mildest winters in Canada, and Vancouver winters are also temperate, with an average of 11 days of snowfall per year. The Okanagan enjoys mild winters with little snowfall. But farther north, things change drastically. Prince George's average low in January, for instance, is –13°C, and the average low for a Fort Nelson in January is a chilly –26°C.

WHISTLER AND BLACKCOMB
The Whistler Blackcomb resort is a true winter wonderland, with 200 ski runs, nearly 40 chairlifts and three glaciers across two mountains. Some of the best powder in North America is accessible by ski lift, heli-ski service or snow cat.

GROUSE MOUNTAIN
Vancouverites looking for quick access to winter sports can look to Grouse Mountain, where skiing, snowshoeing, skating and sleigh rides are only a few minutes and an aerial tram ride away.

DOGSLEDDING
B.C. also offers ample opportunity for the dogsledding enthusiast, from former Gold Rush country around Salmo to all-day excursions around Bridge Lake.

"SANDBLASTING"
Skiers who can't wait for the next snowfall can take heart: "Sandblasting" is a unique summer sport practised near Prince George. Essentially, you "ski" down the slopes of the sandy Nechako cutbanks. And yes, that's on skis. The cutbanks were the setting of the annual Prince George Sandblast Competition until the high rate of accidents caused its cancellation.

◀ **Joffre Group** The Peak of Mount Matier rises behind mountaineers' tents northeast of Lillooet.

◀ **Mount Alan Campbell** A skier shreds through the trees near the Campbell Icefields Chalet.

◀◀ **Campbell Icefield** Accessible by helicopter, the Campbell Icefields Chalet offers dedicated skiers a warm place to stay while they ski the epic slopes nearby.

▲ **Pigeon Spire** Climbers hike along the west ridge of the spire, which lies between the Vowell and Bugaboo glaciers.

▶▶ **Kootenays Region** Skiers on a trail leading from Valkyr Hut in the Selkirk Mountains.

Escape to Bella Coola

Gordon Baron & Cindy Phillips
PHOTOGRAPHERS

STRETCHING FROM CENTRAL BRITISH COLUMBIA TO THE OUTER MID-COAST ISLANDS IN THE PACIFIC, THIS RUGGED AND REMOTE AREA IS HOME TO TWO BIG PARKS: TWEEDSMUIR PROVINCIAL PARK AND THE HAKAI LUXVBALIS CONSERVANCY AREA. IT'S ALSO ONE OF CANADA'S LAST TRUE FRONTIERS, WHERE ANIMALS AND SEA LIFE OUTNUMBER PEOPLE.

The Bella Coola region of B.C. is secluded and untamed, and by land or sea, in winter or summer, it is an amazingly diverse world unto itself—it's one of those beautiful places you have to see to believe.

In just one hour, you can descend from alpine meadows 1,524 metres above sea level, right down into the lush, temperate old-growth rainforest below. The Alexander Mackenzie Heritage Trail runs between Quesnel and Bella Coola, and it's popular for horseback riding, hiking and backpacking. The British Columbia Ferry Corporation operates a passenger service, connecting the fishing villages of Bella Coola, Bella Bella and Klemtu to Vancouver Island and the lower mainland.

About 115 kilometres southwest of Bella Coola, you'll find another treasure of the region: B.C.'s largest marine park. Accessible by sea or air, the Hakai Luxvbalis Conservancy Area is home to white-sand beaches, secret lagoons and remote islands. In summer, outdoor enthusiasts fly in for the legendary fishing, boaters enjoy the beaches and safe anchorages, and passengers aboard cruise ships marvel at the stunning scenery.

Winter is especially spectacular because it's storm and hurricane season on the outer Pacific islands. The outer islands act as shields, spewing water and spray 30 metres into the air as waves crash into them with awesome power. The force of this motion snaps logs like toothpicks. Centuries of relentless pounding has taken its toll on the battered shorelines. Small inland waterways have formed. Rocks have broken free from the jagged granite cliffs above, and roll back and forth along the shore with each ocean swell. Trees have been stunted and twisted by the wind into bonsai shapes, creating a stunning backdrop.

The Cariboo Chilcotin Coast is a rugged paradise with a wealth of history, culture, adventure and hospitality. This coastline is our greatest escape in Canada, and we're privileged to call this wondrous area home.

◄ **North Bentic Arm** The historic B.C. Packers' Clover Leaf cannery still stands today, and is used for storing and repairing fishermen's nets.

▲ **Hakai Luxvbalis Conservancy Area** A white-sand beach opens onto the Pacific, giving visitors a glimpse of paradise.

▶ **Pruth Bay** The sailing ship *Pacific Grace* at anchor.

▶▶ **Thornsen Creek** An ancient stone petroglyph. Some of the petroglyphs are thousands of years old.

▼ **New Westminster** A full moon shines down on the Pattullo Bridge and neighbouring Skybridge, both of which span the Fraser River.

▼▼ **Cariboo** The Sheep Creek Bridge crosses the Fraser River just west of Williams Lake.

▶ **North Vancouver** The Capilano Suspension Bridge that spans the Capilano Canyon and River opened in the late 1800s. Today, it's a tourist attraction and gateway to the canyon's many recreation facilities.

▼ **Vancouver** This zigzag bridge in the VanDusen Botanical Garden offers visitors a quiet spot to get away from city life.

▼▼ **Hell's Gate** The Hell's Gate Bridge spans a particularly dramatic stretch of the Fraser River.

Bridges

▲ **Vancouver** The downtown core makes a dramatic backdrop to the memorial to track and field star Harry Jerome in Stanley Park.

"It is wonderful to feel the grandness of Canada in the raw, not because she is Canada but because she's something sublime that you were born into, some great rugged power that you are a part of."

—Emily Carr

◀ **Mount Robson Provincial Park**
A clear view of Mount Robson's south face. The mountain is the highest in the Canadian Rockies.

▼▼ **Penticton** Sun-soaked bathers tubing down the Penticton Channel.

▼ **Kamloops** An umbrella makes a playful splash of red against a meadow in the Central Interior region.

Gone Fishing

David Lambroughton
PHOTOGRAPHER

IN FALL, THE SKEENA AREA EXPLODES WITH COLOUR AND THE ARGUMENT IN MY HEAD ABOUT WHETHER TO PICK UP MY ROD OR MY CAMERA IS AT ITS GREATEST.

At the age of 12, I was already a keen fisherman; so when my dad bought me my first fly rod, the deal was sealed. I loved fly-fishing—studying the aquatic insects and tying flies to look like them. A lifetime journey had begun.

I'd spread out a large map of B.C. on the kitchen table and fantasize about all the trips I wanted to make. Forty-five fishing seasons later, I'm still staring at the same map—there are more rivers and lakes than you could ever visit in a lifetime.

April is when the murmur begins: But if I had to choose my favourite month for trout fishing it would be July, when the spring runoff is over and the river levels drop. This is the time to fish the rivers that drain the western slope of the Rockies. Fishing my way up a small stream, surrounded by stunning scenery, and dropping dry flies into all the pools and pockets is nirvana to me.

In late July, I'll get a phone call from a fishing pal, telling me that it's time to head west to the island! Summer run steelhead can be found in most rivers that drain the west coast of Vancouver Island. Some days all you get from scrambling over boulders and bush-bashing around canyons are cuts and bruises.

Later, in August, the steelhead head up the Skeena to her famous tributaries that are the largest of their kind. The anglers you most often meet are tight-lipped veterans who take special care with the steelhead they hook, leaving them some water when they are gently unhooked so they never touch the dry rocks.

As you fish your way down the pools and runs, you are fishing though personal history, remembering the many big fish and great friends with whom you shared the river. And, as your swinging fly comes to a stop and a fish is in the air, you remember why you came.

▶ **Chilcotin District**
A beautiful specimen of rainbow trout from the Chilko River.

▶▶ **Vancouver Island**
Fishing for summer run steelhead.

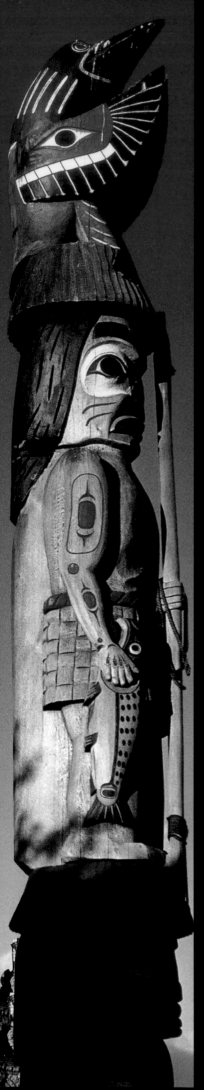

◄◄ **Vancouver** The Knowledge Totem Pole stands on the grounds of B.C.'s legislature. It was carved by Coast Salish artist Cicero August, and represents the oral traditions of the province's First Nations peoples.

◄ **Quatsino Sound** A salmon farm near the north end of Vancouver Island.

▼ **Vancouver** The downtown skyline looms over a cricket match in Stanley Park.

▲ **North Bentick Arm**
The old Tallheo Cannery
still stands opposite the
town of Bella Coola.
Nowadays, it's an inn
that serves legions of
outdoors enthusiasts
every year.

◄ **Rossland** Snow-
covered evergreens are
good news indeed to
skiers at the Red
Mountain Resort.

"Our hopes are high.
Our faith in the people is great.
Our courage is strong.
And our dreams for this
beautiful country will never die."

—Pierre Elliott Trudeau

THE WEST

"ON THE PRAIRIES, THERE ARE HORSES, BADLANDS AND OIL; FIELDS OF COLOURFUL CROPS, GRAVEL ROADS, LONG DISTANCES AND WIDE-OPEN SPACES; ENORMOUS STAR FILLED SKIES; AND WIND— ALWAYS THE WIND, PLAYING THE SONG OF THE PRAIRIES."

—BRIAN CURTIS

◄ **Lake Louise, Alberta**
The crystal blue glacial lake, located in the heart of Banff National Park, is named after Princess Louise Caroline Alberta, daughter of Queen Victoria.

The West is a Place to Call Home

Brian Curtis

As I ponder what the Canadian Prairies mean to me, I am overwhelmed by positive emotions and happy memories. Everything comes back, for me, to the simple fact that I love it here. It is familiar and comfortable and safe here. It is beautiful and big.

As a child, I walked many miles on frozen gravel roads, my boots playing a crunchy cadence. I skated in a million hockey games on the frozen sloughs of my small town—going home long after it was time—my frozen face covered with frosty wind-tears and white breath—toes, lips and fingers unfeeling until the inevitable tingly thaw.

In my youth I ran wild, travelling long distances to see girls in tiny towns or looking for the best places to dance, fish or fight. I woke up in the early darkness and drove for hours to hunt in frozen fields and crash through snow covered bush in search of deer. I spent countless hours travelling to watch our football team and I loved every straight-down-the-highway minute of it.

As an adult, I'm still here. I'm still on these prairies, and I still love it. I love the enormous star-filled skies full of planets and strange blinking lights. I love the badlands and the wildlife. I love the changing colours and light; so good for photography, and the people.

Prairie people are those of compassion, honesty, morals and values, and work ethic; people that enjoy preserving history and traditions, people that give, people that can take whatever Mother Nature throws and simply laugh and enjoy this hard-working life on the Canadian Prairies; my kind of people. I love it here.

The Soul of Alberta

Todd Korol
PHOTOGRAPHER

LIGHT SPILLING OFF MOUNTAINS AT SUNRISE. DRAMATIC NIGHT CITYSCAPES.
WIDE OPEN PRAIRIE PLAINS. SPECTACULAR LANDSCAPES AND THE ETHEREAL
QUALITY OF LIGHT COMBINE TO CREATE BREATHTAKING ALBERTA.

▲ **Longview** The foothills of the Rockies swell above Waldron Ranch in southern Alberta.

◀ **Calgary** The Calgary Tower overlooks downtown and the Saddledome.

On one of my first trips to the province (I grew up in Manitoba), I was driving on a gravel road south of Calgary along the Whaleback, a rolling foothills landscape where the light changes as quickly as the weather. Patches of light swept across the swaying grasslands, hawks circled overhead, catching the warmth of the day's rising thermals, and songbirds sang in the distance. Stopping to photograph the breathtaking views, I had to wait only a few minutes for the whole scene to be changed by the light.

The more one travels this province, the more one discovers its secrets. They're generally hidden just off the main highway, down some gravel road. One minute you can be caught in traffic and the next you can find yourself alone in the middle of the prairie with a meadowlark singing you a tune. Drive a few kilometres out of the city and you'll find the soul of Alberta. Kin-

sella, Fort Chipewyan (or "Fort Chip"), Bassano, Picture Butte and two of my favourite places in the world, Milk River and Pincher Creek, are places where the people are proud of their town, their province and the land in which they live.

Almost every June, fellow photographer Mike Drew and I head south to Writing-On-Stone, located on the Milk River just a few kilometres north of Montana, to take in the annual Writing-On-Stone rodeo. We leave Calgary at sun-up, and drive into the grasslands and coulees of southern Alberta. Each year we're rewarded by the perfect light in which to capture amateur rodeo riders getting bucked off horses with great western names...Firefly, Barn Dance and Stormy Weather.

I think everyone remembers the first time he or she ever saw the Rocky Mountains. Driving into the mountains, one can't help but be awestruck by their ruggedness and beauty.

55

► **Edmonton** The North Saskatchewan River runs through the provincial capital.

►► **Banff** The Rocky Mountains tower above the surrounding land near the B.C. border.

▼ **Brocket** Geese fly south over the Oldman River west of Lethbridge.

►▼ **Waterton Lakes National Park** A Buffalo roams the grasslands of the southwest.

Add to that the emerald and blue lakes, and it's easy to see why many Albertans head straight to the mountains, winter or summer.

While I am attracted to southern Alberta for many reasons—light, landscape, people—it's character that draws me to northern Alberta. The character of the landscape, the season and people of the north surprise me around every curve of the road.

I love the northern spirit of adventure. Once I photographed an event called The Muffaloose, a February pilgrimage of brave souls who mountain bike from a spot north of Fort McMurray some 200 kilometres up to a frozen Lake Athabasca and into Fort Chipewyan.

As a photographer, I travel a great deal and have flown around the world more than a few times. One day I was riding my favourite horse, Bingo, south of Pincher Creek, with my good friend Frank Jenkins riding alongside. Frank is a third generation rancher and a man who truly loves who he is and what he does. We were moving his cattle from their winter grounds to summer pastures and enjoying life. The high-noon sun was beating down on us, and to our right the Rocky Mountains provided us with a postcard backdrop.

"Of all those places you've travelled," Frank asked, "what's your favourite?"

I stopped Bingo in his tracks, looked around and stated simply, "I'm in it right now. It doesn't get any better than this."

The Alberta Badlands

East of the Rocky Mountains, Alberta's Red Deer Badlands holds its own for amazing natural attractions. Millions of years of erosion have carved the unusual, almost lunar landscape of the badlands, exposing layer after layer of sedimentary rock and revealing vast, ancient fossil beds.

The Dinosaur Trail The 48-kilometre Dinosaur Trail starts north of Drumheller and heads west along the Red Deer River valley. This "Valley of the Dinosaurs" is a huge prehistoric graveyard where whole skeletons of dinosaurs have been found. Near the end of the trail is Prehistoric Park where life-size dinosaur models are displayed.

The Hoodoo Trail Eerie, vertical sandstone rock formations jutting out of the Red Deer River valley, their odd shapes sculpted by millennia of wind and water erosion, hoodoos are a popular attraction in the badlands. Walk the 2.5-kilometre trail through spectacular examples of hoodoos with hues ranging from subtle pinks to earthy browns, in Writing-on-Stone Provincial Park. This park has a spiritual significance for the Blackfoot people and has been considered a sacred landscape for generations.

RIDE THE WILD WEST
HORSES, BOOTS, CHAPS AND COWBOY HATS

"A cowboy can make riding a horse look poetic."

—Todd Korol

ALBERTA: COWBOY COUNTRY
The prairies have a strong cowboy tradition that dates back to the ranching culture and American immigration at the end of the 19th century. But the impact of the horse goes far beyond the romantic history of the cowboy. Horses played a huge role in opening up the country to trade and settlement, maintaining order and keeping communications alive before the internal combustion engine changed the face of the west. And horses are still very much a part of working ranches today.

▲ **Western Alberta** The Ya Ha Tinda Ranch is a federally-owned facility where horses are raised and trained as mounts for Canada's park wardens.

◄ **Southern Alberta** Mountains loom large behind a rancher in Twin Butte, southwest of Lethbridge.

► **Calgary** A bronco rider is sent flying at the Calgary Stampede.

►► **Turner Valley** An Appaloosa stands out against the fall colours of a field and nearby birch grove.

► **Calgary** Chuckwagon teams charge to the finish line at the Stampede.

▼ **Willow Creek** Ranchers and cattle stop for a well-earned drink at the end of a two-day drive.

THE ROUNDUP

A roundup is the central event of a ranching work cycle and a practical demonstration of legendary cowboy work ethic. It requires a lot of planning (moving cattle, tents, chuck wagons, people, horses and more), and long hours on horseback, in all sorts of weather. It can be dangerous work; fraught with daily hazards. The biggest roundup in Canadian history took place near Fort Macleod, Alberta in 1885. It included over 100 cowboys and 16 chuckwagons moving over 60,000 head of cattle.

CALGARY STAMPEDE—THE GREATEST OUTDOOR SHOW ON EARTH

The Stampede is the world's largest outdoor rodeo, attracting more than one million visitors each year. For ten exciting days, tourists and Albertans, celebrate the time-honoured team of cowboy and horse. It features rodeo competitions, chuckwagon races, First Nations events, pancake breakfasts, concerts and so much more. Each year, the Calgary Stampede Parade, which includes about 5,000 people and 800 horses, kicks off the festival.

59

The Land of Living Skies

John Perret
PHOTOGRAPHER

MY LIFE'S PASSION IS TO CAPTURE SASKATCHEWAN THROUGH MY PHOTOGRAPHY—AND TO SHOW OTHERS HOW AWESOME OUR PRAIRIE PROVINCE IS. YOU CAN'T APPRECIATE IT FROM THE TRANS-CANADA OR THE YELLOWHEAD HIGHWAY. YOU NEED TO GET OFF THE BEATEN PATH.

▲ **Near Craik** Granaries huddled under a Saskatchewan sunset. The roads criss-crossing this province are innumerable, but each carries with it an old story and a new opportunity.

◀ **St. Denis** As in many parts of the province, vast fields of canola stretch to the horion east of Saskatoon.

Saskatchewan is a province built on the strength of its founding citizens, the optimism of their descendants and the hope of today's settlers. Its immigrants came from around the world seeking a place to call home, where they could carve their livelihood from a land rich in agriculture and brimming with promise.

From our founding First Nations, to the young entrepreneurs of today, Saskatchewan has seen some of the greatest tenacity and grit ever shown by human beings. They were fur traders, farmers, builders and businessmen, and they spoke French, Ukrainian, German and Chinese, among other languages.

Some groups, such as the Doukhobors, came seeking freedom from religious persecution. Testament to that freedom can be seen in the numerous churches that dot the province's landscape, where steeples and spires boldly reach up over the crops to the vast prairie sky.

Along with Alberta, Saskatchewan was once part of what was called the North-West Territories. The area gained some notoriety thanks to the 1885 North-West Rebellion led by Louis Riel, and Ottawa's fear that Saskatchewan and Alberta together would have too much power as one large territory led to the current boundaries. In 1905 both Alberta and Saskatchewan took their places in Confederation.

My mother's parents were immigrants of English descent; my father's, French. My father's family homestead was near the town of Duck Lake, across the South Saskatchewan River from Batoche, where the final battle of Riel's North-West Rebellion took place. My father felt a deep connection to the land he'd helped to farm and grew to know so well.

To truly appreciate the wonder of Saskatchewan, you must shun the clichés and resist the stereotypes. It is not terra nullius.

61

▶ **Smuts** Storm clouds descend upon Pryma Church, one of the province's many Ukrainian Catholic churches.

▼ **Big Muddy Badlands** This rippling landscape in the south is green for only a short time in the spring.

▼▼ **Unity** Winter winds sculpt huge snowdrifts around prairie buildings in winter.

It's a place diverse in its landscapes, majestic in its extremes and never boring.

Whether you talk about farming, landscapes, weather or culture, seasonal diversity is Saskatchewan's hallmark. Given the array of lakes and rivers to travel, summer is undeniably a tourist's favourite season in Saskatchewan, but the northern forests are spectacular in the fall. And the harsh landscape of winter brings out shapes and colours not visible when the trees have leaves. I love to photograph lightning storms or fog, at sunrise or sunset, and in –60°C wind chill when the air feels like thorns in your skin.

For a photographer, light and colour are lifeblood. This is "the land of living skies," and the skies we enjoy on the prairies are unequalled for offering up different colours of light at different times of the year or the day.

In the summer, my excursions often begin before sunrise. The landscape may be clear or drenched in fog and dew. Sometimes I encounter animals on the way—deer, moose, coyotes, foxes and owls. Then the sun will peek over the horizon's edge. This is what I have come for. The golden light begins to catch the contours of the hills and still hides the valleys—light against darkness. When there is fog or mist the sun comes up like a golden disk, its intensity subdued by the mist. The golden light illuminates the Saskatchewan landscape for a few perfect moments and then the drama is over until the evening's sunset.

▲ **Rosetown** A vast field of golden mature wheat awaits harvest.

◄ **Lake Diefenbaker** Sailboats moor in a tranquil harbour. The lake formed in the 1960s when the Gardiner Dam was built on the South Saskatchewan River near Elbow.

▶ **Aberdeen** There are fewer than 200 old-style prairie grain elevators left in Saskatchewan today.

URBAN PRAIRIE
FRIENDLY NEIGHBOURHOODS, SPECTACULAR SCENERY

"Edmonton isn't really the end of the world—although you can see it from there."
—Ralph Klein

EDMONTON

The capital of Alberta, the city is famous for its West Edmonton Mall and for hosting the largest fringe theatre festival in North America. Shoppers and nightlife lovers can't do better than Whyte Avenue, which offers a lively pub and club scene as well as trendy shopping. Attractions in the greater area include whimsical delights such as the world's biggset pysanka (decorated Easter egg) in Vegreville, the world's biggest perogy in Glendon, and the world's first UFO landing in St. Paul.

CALGARY

Calgary is the epicentre of Canada's petroleum industry, but it is also an ethnically diverse city with a large Chinatown, a Little Italy and several other culturally-rich areas. Cowboys can git along to the Calgary Stampede, while movie buffs can enjoy the Calgary Film Festival.

SASKATOON

Settled by the Temperance Colonization Society in the late 1800s, this city got its name from the Cree name for a local berry. It now has seven bridges across the South Saskatchewan River, a busy airport and several colleges and universities. Saskatoon has large First Nations and Métis populations.

WINNIPEG

Winnipeggers are both arts-savvy and diverse, and the city has a lot going on: Great museums, the famous Royal Winnipeg Ballet, entertaining festivals and excellent cuisine. Winnipeggers come from many ethnic backgrounds, and the St. Boniface area is an important centre for western French Canadian culture.

▲ **Winnipeg** The Manitoba legislature glows in the colours of fall against a backdrop of the downtown core.

▶ **Calgary** Alberta's biggest city is the epicentre of Canada's oil industry.

◀ **Saskatoon** The northern lights glow above the Saskatoon skyline.

they can take it."

June Callwood

◄ **Drumheller, Alberta** Lightning flashes above the hoodoos that tower over Alberta's badlands.

▲ **Chin, Alberta** A lone horse stands guard before grain elevators near Lethbridge.

Animals

◀ **Winnipeg** A white-tailed doe at the FortWhyte Alive environmental education centre.

▼ **Edson, Alberta** A beaver finds nourishment in a creek.

▼▼ **Carroll, Manitoba** A fox suns himself in the grass.

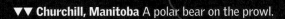

▶ Red Deer, Alberta
A weasel finds a sturdy branch from which to perch.

▼ Calgary A family of prairie dogs out for a stroll in Fish Creek Provincial Park.

▼▼ Churchill, Manitoba A polar bear on the prowl.

▶ Southern Saskatchewan Hardy Welsh cattle have been introduced, in part, because they can endure prairie winters.

▼ Winnipeg Bison at the FortWhyte Alive environmental education centre.

Heartland of Manitoba

David Reede

PHOTOGRAPHER

EARLY EACH SPRING THE PRAIRIE CROCUS—THE FLORAL EMBLEM OF MANITOBA—POKES ITS BLOOMS ABOVE THE COLD SOIL. DESPITE PERIODS OF SNOW AND COLD WEATHER, IT GROWS AND FLOURISHES UNDAUNTED. THAT ENDURANCE TYPIFIES THE SPIRIT AND THE POSITIVE ATTITUDE OF MANITOBANS.

▲ **Winnipeg** The Red River flows gently through the downtown core.

◄ **Duck Mountain Provincial Park** Fishing for walleye in southwestern Manitoba.

As a transplanted Maritimer, the first thing that I noticed about Manitoba was the wide open prairie sky broken only by small towns with towering grain elevators. On a summer's day the sky is filled with puffy white clouds, and the seemingly endless patterns of yellows, greens and blues created by a multitude of crops such as alfalfa, canola, flax and wheat add interest to a sweeping landscape.

Manitoba is a land of vast lakes created by glacial meltwaters, expanses of forest hugged by gently rolling farmland and windswept shorelines along Hudson Bay that are inhabited by polar bears during part of the year.

Winnipeg, the capital and largest city, was established where the turbid waters of the Assiniboine River empty into the Red River. This spot where the rivers meet is called The Forks, and it has been a meeting place for people for thousands of years—first natives, and later, Metis and European settlers. Today it is frequented by city folks and tourists alike.

Quaint communities dot the farming regions of Manitoba. Agriculture dominates the land and creates a yearly cycle. In spring, huge tractors disturb the soil and plant the crops. Late spring and early summer bring on the lush greens and vibrant colours of crops growing and flowering. By late summer and early fall, large combines trawl the landscape amid a sea of golden wheat and barley, kicking up dust to bring in the harvest.

Autumn is short-lived and winter, which brings harsh north winds and snow, usually lasts from early November to late March. Like many Manitobans, I see great beauty in clear and crisp winter days. Sometimes, with temperatures hovering at –30°C and hoarfrost on the trees, I'll spend most of my day outside, documenting the beauty of the landscape. Often the wind carves intricate patterns in the snow as it roams across the open prairie.

Manitoba's size and the variety of its landscapes provide unique spots to visit. One of

▶ **Pisew Falls Provincial Park** The Grass River surges 13 metres down the province's second highest waterfall.

▼ **Grande Pointe** Autumn light bathes pumpkins on a farm near Winnipeg.

▲ **Winnipeg** Two girls catch critters at a pond near the Royal Canadian Mint.

▶ **Brandon** Canola and spring wheat coexist in the scenic Tiger Hills.

▶▶ **Dufresne** A bounty of straw bales dot a farm in southern Manitoba.

the most interesting in the south is the Tiger Hills area, with its gently rolling hills and crop patterns. The region was created when the glaciers retreated and left behind hilly deposits of debris called moraines. Not far from Tiger Hills is the Spirit Sands, a semidesert area also created by glacial deposits.

For a number of years, I fished in the north in many lakes and streams. It is very fulfilling to sit around a campfire alongside a pristine lake, eating freshly caught walleye and watching the northern lights dance across the sky. Much of northern Manitoba is inaccessible by road and is the domain of the float plane.

Each of the province's many provincial and national parks has its own unique ecosystem. My favourites include Duck Mountain, Whiteshell and Pisew Falls provincial parks. Whiteshell, on the edge of the rugged Canadian Shield about a 90-minute drive east of Winnipeg, contains abundant wildlife and petroforms—stones laid out in various forms by the early native peoples. Duck Mountain Provincial Park is on the other side of the province and straddles the Saskatchewan border. Baldy Mountain is located here; at 831 metres above sea level, it's the highest point in Manitoba. And at Pisew Falls Provincial Park in the north, the Grass River tumbles 13 metres over bedrock, then flows down a gorge. To be at the bottom of the falls at sunrise in summer is truly refreshing.

▲ **Saskatchewan** First Nations dancers at a powwow.

◀ **Churchill River, Saskatchewan** Camping on a sandbar in northern Saskatchewan.

▼ **Banff National Park, Alberta** A park warden on boundary patrol near the Panther River.

◀ ▼ **Dapp, Alberta** A cowboy on a beautiful Arabian leads the Canada Day parade in this small community north of Edmonton.

◀ **Saskatoon** Fiddling and blowing on the mouth harp at the Saskatoon Fringe Theatre Festival.

▼ **La Broquerie, Manitoba** Members of the Southeastern Manitoba Draft Horse Association thresh oats on an overcast September afternoon.

◀ **Pincher Creek, Alberta** A Hutterite girl adds a touch of colour to the sky during the annual Children of the Wind Kite Festival.

▼ **Saskatoon** Colourful and lively Ukrainian dance at the September 2005 centenary.

> "If some countries have too much history, we have too much geography. "
>
> William Lyon Mackenzie King

▼ **Western Alberta** The dramatic landscape of the Rockies offers some of the most beautiful views in western Canada. Parks like Banff and Jasper offer skiing, hiking and canoeing, while campgrounds and cabins are fabulous for getting away for a weekend or a whole summer.

▶ **Northwest Saskatchewan** A huge sand dune near Lake Athabasca. Some of these dunes can reach 30 metres in height and stretch for more than a kilometre.

CENTRAL CANADA

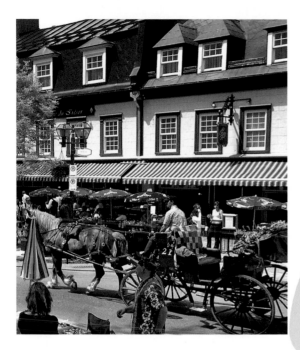

Central Canada is Central to Me

Gary George

When I was 17, back in the mid-70s, I decided to leave my home in Montreal and thumb my way out west—to see the country, assert my independence and hopefully make some cash. I never made it out of Ontario. That's how big and beautiful the province is.

Ontario—from its vineyards and fruit belt to its lunar-like mining regions and mind-blowing lakes and water-ways, left lasting memories. So did the world-class metropolis that is Toronto and our stately, ever-green and much-storied national capital—all worth visiting again and again. And I have over the years.

I returned to Montreal and settled down—to a wife, an education, a career and two kids. Many of my fellow anglo Montrealers were uprooting theirs. The steady stream down Highway 401 eventually became an exodus that swept up two of my three sisters and a few cousins to boot. So, family visits and excursions into Ontario became part of regular life, with the parklands near Long Sault, High-way 2 past Cornwall, Williamstown and Ottawa's Rideau Canal being frequent destinations.

I'm thankful that I returned to Montreal. It has always been home to me, I grew up here. My favourite vacation of all time was a motorcycle ride around the Gaspé peninsula, with its death-defying cliffside views and the howling winds coming in off the Atlantic at Forillon National Park.

I've come to appreciate that most of my neighbours—regardless of their mother tongue, ethnicity, religion or lifestyle—essentially want the same thing I do: to live and raise their families in health, peace and relative comfort.

And I'm sure the same holds true for folks in Ontario. After all, we're neighbours—part of that culturally diverse, naturally beautiful, economic powerhouse known as Central Canada.

"I ALSO REMEMBER TORONTO AS A PLACE WHERE I WAS ABLE TO PURSUE MANY OF MY PERSONAL INTERESTS, RANGING FROM SPORTS TO CULTURAL ACTIVITIES. ONE OF MY MOST MARKING MEMORIES (BESIDES PARTICIPATING IN THE ANNUAL CLIMBING OF THE CN TOWER STAIRS) WAS THE PRIVILEGE OF SINGING WITH THE TAFELMUSIK BAROQUE ORCHESTRA THROUGHOUT MY ENTIRE STAY."
—JULIE PAYETTE

◀ **Niagara Falls** The Horseshoe Falls plunge 52 metres into the Niagara River, which is 56 metres deep at the base of the falls.

The Soul of Ontario

Mike Grandmaison
PHOTOGRAPHER

THERE IS NO SHORTAGE OF SPECTACULAR SCENERY AND HISTORICAL GEMS TO VISIT IN ONTARIO.
IF YOU HAVEN'T BEEN THERE YET, IT'S TIME YOU SAW THIS AWESOME PLACE FOR YOURSELF!

Sudbury is my hometown. I grew up there in the 1950s and learned to appreciate the outdoors during fishing and hiking trips with my family, then later while studying biology at Sudbury's Laurentian University. Though I've been living in Winnipeg for the past 19 years, I make pilgrimages—sometimes as many as four or five a year!—to my home province, either to visit or on a photography assignment.

Before I left Sudbury, I witnessed a remarkable "greening" of the area that began in the early 1970s, led by dedicated scientists in the community. Since then, I've seen the evolution of one of the world's best science centres. Science North focuses on the relationship between science and everyday life in a fun and exciting way.

Ontario's spectacular and diverse scenery seems endless. An hour-and-a-half drive southwest of Sudbury is Killarney Provincial Park. Considered by many to be Ontario's jewel, Killarney is known for its hiking and outstanding beauty, particularly along the shoreline of Lake Huron.

On the Niagara Escarpment, opportunities to capture postcard perfect images abound. As well as the world-famous Niagara Falls, there are smaller, lesser-known, but nonetheless spectacular waterfalls. On the cliffs of the Escarpment are millennium-aged trees, the oldest in eastern North America.

My visits to southern Ontario have always been rewarded with extensive historical richness, including the famous covered bridge ("Kissing Bridge") of West Montrose. A little farther west is the village of St. Jacobs, where Mennonites still travel in horse-drawn carriages. This is also farming country, and touring its extensive fields of corn and soybeans, dairy farms, and old and new barns, is a humbling reminder of the province's agricultural strength.

Most of Ontario's 12 million residents live in southern Ontario. A multitude of attractions, including museums, festivals, parks and shops, entice visitors in quaint small communities and fast-paced large cities.

North of Toronto is the Muskoka region and its beautiful forests and lakes. For many urbanites, this is cottage country, where folks gather on weekends and holidays for rest and

◀ **Hamilton** Coneflower sentinels stand guard over the city from atop the Niagara Escarpment.

◀ **St. Jacobs** A horse-drawn buggy in Western Ontario's Mennonite country.

▼ **Trillium** Ontario's floral emblem.

▼▼ **Lake Superior** A calm winter sunrise near Rossport.

Niagara Peninsula

From Hamilton to the mighty cascade of Niagara Falls, the Niagara Peninsula is one of Canada's richest regions. The peninsula resounded with the clash of American and British arms during the War of 1812. Settled by Quakers, Loyalists, Mennonites and Huguenots, the region has a mild climate and fertile soil, which has made it Canada's fruit belt and major wine-producing region. There are approximately 40 wineries in the Niagara Peninsula Viticultural Area. Other attractions in the region include Niagara Falls, the charming and historic village of Niagara-on-the-Lake, Fort Erie—where guides dressed in period costume recreate a British garrison at the old fort, Grimsby and Port Colborne. The scenery throughout the peninsula is striking in May, when the cherry, peach and apple trees burst into blossom.

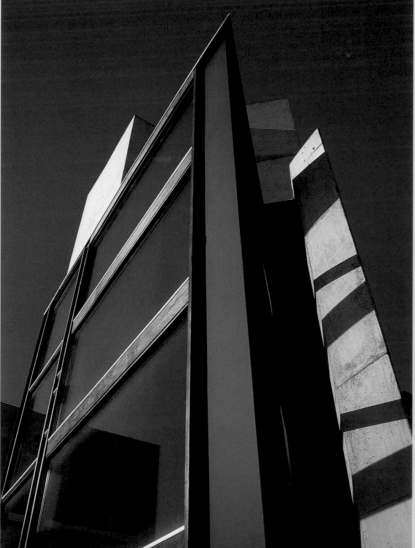

▶ **Waterloo** The angles of the Canadian Clay & Glass Gallery seem to slice the sky. The gallery features works by local and international artists.

▲▲ **Lake Rosseau** Fall colours loom over a waterfront chalet in the Muskoka region.

▲ **Lake of the Bays** Muskoka chairs mind the dock.

recreation. Can you think of anything more relaxing than sipping your morning coffee on the porch with mist rising over the lake and the cry of loons in the distance?

The Muskoka region is also popular with photographers, who venture here in autumn when the forests explode into a tapestry of colours unmatched in the natural world.

A short distance to the east is Algonquin Provincial Park—arguably Ontario's most famous park—renowned for its canoeing and wilderness. It was here that the Group of Seven's Tom Thomson painted the vast expanse of maple hills, rocky ridges, spruce bogs and quiet lakes. The Ontario landscape became an important theme in the artists' paintings that celebrate the extensive rugged beauty of Canada.

Farther north and farther west, Ontario becomes more wild. That's the wilderness country I love—Shield country, where rocky outcrops dot the landscape and where you might, on a clear night, witness a display of the awe-inspiring northern lights.

The shores of Lake Superior, the world's largest freshwater lake—indeed, its water could fill all the other Great Lakes, plus three additional Lake Eries!—offers some of the finest scenery anywhere in this country. It's a harsh, rugged landscape, where the highway often hugs the shoreline as you drive up and over immense hills into the vast wilderness.

▲ **Niagara Falls** The Whirlpool Aero Car is an antique cable car that offers passengers a glorious view of the Niagara Whirlpool below.

▶ **London** Downtown glitters at night.

COSMOPOLITAN TORONTO
CENTRE OF COMMERCE, CAPITAL OF CULTURE

▼ **Toronto** The CN Tower and SkyDome give Toronto one of the most recognizable skylines in Canada.

▲ **Chinatown** Storefronts and colourful signs show off the special character of Toronto's amazing Chinatown, one of the largest on the continent.

▶▲ **Toronto Streetcars** Unique in Canada, streetcars have had a resurgence in interest in recent years.

▶ **Riverdale Farm** Island House is a remnant from the old Riverdale Zoo, which occupied the farm grounds from 1894 to 1974.

"Toronto is a kind of New York operated by the Swiss."

—Peter Ustinov

TORONTO—BIG DADDY OF CANADIAN CITIES

Sitting on the shore of Lake Ontario, Toronto is Canada's most populous city, and fifth largest municipality in North America. It's an economic powerhouse and consistently rated as one of the world's most livable cities by the *Economist Intelligence Unit*. It also has fabulous museums, great theatre and a music scene that simply pops. From its Distillery District and Little Portugal to the vibrant scenes of Queen Street and Kensington Market, Toronto is a town that's always on the go, and ready to be enjoyed.

A GLOBAL METROPOLIS

As a centre of immigration, Toronto's has many ethnic neighbourhoods, including a Greektown, Little Italy and a large Chinatown. The earliest Chinese community can be traced back to the 1870s. Despite the quotas placed on Chinese immigration with the introduction of the Chinese Immigration Act of 1885, Chinatown grew. Today, many say it is the second largest Asian community in North America. Extending along Spadina and Dundas St. West, it's home to businesses that reflect the diversity of Asian cultures and cuisine, including Vietnamese and Thai.

TORONTO'S STREETCARS

Streetcars are not only a good, exhaust-free way of moving people around, they are a symbol of the city: Toronto has the only remaining streetcar system in Canada.

YONGE—LONGEST STREET IN THE WORLD

Yonge Street is one of Toronto's main traffic arteries and is considered by some to be the longest street in the world. First surveyed in 1793 by Lt. Col. John Graves Simcoe, who named it after Sir George Yonge, the Secretary of War, the first 55-kilometre section was built in 1796. Today, Yonge runs north from downtown Toronto, then follows Highway 11 to the Minnesota border. Its length measures approximately 1,896 kilometres.

Ottawa: The Place to Be July First

Frank H. Scheme

PHOTOGRAPHER

EVERY YEAR, THOUSANDS OF PEOPLE POUR INTO OTTAWA FOR CANADA DAY. WHAT BETTER PLACE TO CELEBRATE OUR GREAT LAND AND SHARED HERITAGE THAN OUR NATION'S CAPITAL!

Ottawa's open green spaces, lush parks, tree-lined boulevards, endless bicycle paths and excellent walking trails make it a special place for anyone who loves the outdoors. For those of us who enjoy nights out on the town, there are festivals for every season of the year, charitable fundraisers and gala events that attract thousands of people in support of worthy causes. And last but certainly not least, Ottawa's magnificent architecture and historic landmarks are on display at every turn, standing in silent tribute to Ottawa's standing as a multi-faceted, multicultural urban centre, of which all Canadians can be justifiably proud.

It is said that long before the arrival of the French and English, the Algonquins lived in the area near the Kichesippi— the Great River. When the French arrived, they renamed the river La Rivière des Outaouais, after the Outaouais tribe. In the mid-18th century, when the region came under British rule, the waterway became known as the Ottawa River. In 1826, Lt.-Col. John By was appointed commanding royal engineer and was commissioned to design and build a 200-kilometre canal that would be used to transport munitions between Montreal and the western part of the country. The next year, as the massive project that would become one of Ottawa's hallmarks was getting under way, the settlement where By made his headquarters became known as Bytown. By 1836, steamboat traffic was moving along the Ottawa River and the canal. Fuelled by the area's growing lumber trade, the bustling community of Bytown was incorporated in 1855 and its name was changed to Ottawa. Queen Victoria proclaimed the city as the new seat of government in 1857 and construction of the Parliament Buildings on Barrick Hill began two years later.

Disaster struck Ottawa in 1900 when a fire, which started in Hull (formerly Wright's Town), burned large segments of that city. Fanned by high winds, it spread across the river and destroyed much of Ottawa's industrial core. Seven people died, more than 3,000 homes were lost and property damage was estimated at $100 million. Sixteen years later, fire broke out in Parliament's Centre Block; all that was left were its outer walls. Reconstruction began almost immediately, following plans designed by Jean-Omer Marchand, and was finally completed in 1922.

In the 1950s, a "Greenbelt" was established around Ottawa to protect rural land from urban sprawl. An idea first put forward by renowned architect Jacques Gréber as part of a comprehensive plan to create a distinctive setting for the nation's capital, the Greenbelt runs in a 45-kilometre arc, encompassing a mix of farmland, forest and wetlands on the city's outskirts. The greenery is enjoyed by all.

Ottawa has embraced its role as a cultural and heritage showcase by staging such popular

◀ **Governor General's Foot Guards** The regiment does ceremonial guard duties, along with the Canadian Grenadier Guards and Cavalry Squadron of the Governor General's Horse Guards.

▲ **Rideau Canal** The gothic revival grace of the Parliament Buildings make a picturesque backdrop for boating and strolling on the canal in summer.

◄ **Royal Canadian Mounted Police** Riders escort the Governor General's carriage to Parliament Hill.

▲ **ByWard Market** Even baskets of fruit get the patriotic treatment on July 1st.

▶ **History on Parade** Native attire is proudly on display for Canada Day. Cultures, from the First Nations to Ottawa's vibrant communities, bring a multi-ethnic flavour to the birthday festivities.

annual events as Canada Day in the Capital, Winterlude, a tulip festival and jazz and blues festivals. The National Arts Centre is home to a world-class orchestra and plays host to artists from Canada and around the world. The National Gallery of Canada was completed in 1988, followed by the Canadian Museum of Civilization, designed by Native architect Douglas Cardinal. A recent addition is the new war museum on LeBreton Flats, a fitting tribute to Canada's armed forces.

Canada Day festivities are highlighted by an outdoor show in front of the Parliament Buildings, presided over by the Governor General and prime minister. In the National Arts Centre, a concert comprising hundreds of young singers in choirs from all over the country take part in "Unisong," featuring Canadian music. In downtown Ottawa and the ByWard Market, street drummers, buskers, artists and musicians entertain a sea of people, many decked out in Canada-themed costumes. A roar never fails to rise from the gathered crowd as the Snowbirds perform their traditional fly-past. The party goes on well into the night, culminating with a fabulous display of fireworks.

Birds

▶ **Montreal** A great blue heron browses at the water's edge.

▶ **Guelph, Ontario** A Canada goose keeps a careful watch over a gosling on Guelph Lake.

▲ **St-Valliers, Quebec** A snowy owl soars in search of prey.

▲ **Barrie** Seagulls huddle against a sudden winter snowfall.

MONTREAL—A DISTINCT SOCIETY
WITH A MULTICULTURAL HEART AND SOUL

▲ **Mary, Queen of the World Cathedral** The third largest church in Quebec pays homage to St. Peter's Basilica in Rome.

▼ **Old Port of Montreal** Four lakers moored at Montreal's port. Behind, a full moon sets over the city.

"I'm a Quebecker, I was born alienated."

—Laurier LaPierre

NO LONGER TWO SOLITUDES

Though the city's official language is French, life in Montreal happens in a plethora of languages. This polyglot character has become an integral part of Montreal's civic culture, inspiring not only a pulsating arts scene, but also giving the city an enviable place on the international stage. Montreal enjoys the status of being Canada's second largest city and the third-largest French-speaking city in the world (after Paris and Kinshasa).

ERUDITE AND SOPHISTICATED

Within an eight-kilometre radius of downtown Montreal, there are six universities and twelve junior colleges, giving it the highest concentration of post-secondary students of all North American cities (followed by Boston).

MONTREAL'S UNDERGROUND

Beneath its busy streets lies an attraction that is unique in North America: an underground city. A double-decker maze connects downtown buildings, Metro stations and shopping malls, and it is the largest underground complex in the world. Over 32 kilometres of passageways conjoin 1,700 boutiques, businesses, hotels and more. In winter, 500,000 people use the underground city daily.

VIBRANT LIFESTYLE

Tourists love to explore Montreal's club scenes: on Crescent Street; the French sensibilities of the cafés and bars on St-Denis; bohemian St-Laurent Boulevard—all show Montreal's bubbling cultural character. Some of the best people-watching is in Old Montreal or in the Plateau district, home to many of Montreal's artists and musicians. It is also widely considered that Montreal has some of the finest restaurants in North America.

◀ **Olympic Stadium** Built to support a retractable roof, the Big O's tower is the world's tallest inclined structure.

▲▲ **Rue Laval** Some of Montreal's beautiful old houses are painted in a very Montreal array of colours.

▲ **Parc Jeanne-Mance** A romantic moment on a beautiful summer afternoon.

▲ **Sudbury, Ontario** The slag heaps at the Creighton Nickel
Mine become mountains of fire at night as the white-hot
slag lights up their flanks. During the day, smokestacks jut into
the sky above an almost lunar landscape.

"Well the girls are out to bingo,
And the boys are gettin' stinko,

▲ ▲ **Îles de la Madeleine, Quebec** The sedimentary rock at Parc de Gros-Cap is covered with a thin layer of iron oxide, which produces its vibrant colour.

◀ **Gatineau, Quebec** The Canadian Museum of Civilization was designed by renowned architect Douglas Cardinal to reflect the curves of the nearby Ottawa River. The museum sits near the bridge that joins Ottawa and Gatineau.

▲ **Toronto** The BAPS Shri Swaminarayan Mandir was completed in 2007, without the use of structural steel. It was built using more than 6,000 tons of hand-carved marble, limestone, sandstone and wood.

FESTIVAL NATION
PASSIONATE AND SPIRITED

"The heart never knows the colour of the skin."

—Chief Dan George

Central Canada loves its festivals. Throughout the year, music fests, literary feasts, theatre festivals and winter carnivals keep Canadians and tourists jumping. It's a year-long party.

MONTREAL INTERNATIONAL JAZZ FESTIVAL
People come out in droves to experience the world's largest festival of its kind; young and old brave the sweltering heat of a Montreal summer to dance, sing and otherwise enjoy world-class jazz music from the likes of Pat Metheny, George Benson and Diana Krall.

JUST FOR LAUGHS
In 1983, Gilbert Rozon tried to bring the gift of laughter to as many people as possible when he launched the Just For Laughs Festival. More than twenty-five years later, it's still going strong. Nearly 2,000 artists and over 2 million people have taken part in the event.

OTTAWA BLUESFEST
Born in 1994, the national capital's annual July festival has attracted blues giants Buddy Guy, Ray Charles and Etta James—and thousands of appreciative fans.

GAY PRIDE
Pride Week in Toronto is one of the largest Pride celebrations in the world. It features ten days of world class arts and cultural programming, community activities, one of the world's largest street festivals and more.

CARIBANA
Toronto's Caribbean carnival is the largest in North America. It features calypso, steel pan and a parade showcasing an incredible display of colour and pageantry.

TORONTO INTERNATIONAL FILM FESTIVAL (TIFF)
TIFF ranks among the most prestigious international film festivals. For ten days, filmmakers and film aficionados watch the best in new cinema, and the festival attracts Canadian and international industry professionals, including major Hollywood stars.

◄ **Powwow** Every August sees Manitoulin Island's Wikwemikong First Nation host a fabulous powwow. There are others virtually every weekend throughout the summer in most parts of Canada.

▼ **Music** A trumpeter sets the mood as night descends upon Montreal.

▲ **Montreal International Jazz Festival** Music lovers shrug off the June heat for one of this famous fest's many free concerts.

◄◄ **Toronto International Film Festival** One of the world's premiere film festivals, the TIFF is where many studios hope the Oscar buzz for their films begins.

◄ **Caribana** A reveller celebrates Islands culture during Toronto's huge annual Caribbean bash.

Sanctuaries

◀ **Bonaventure Island, Quebec** Northern gannets flock to this island bird sanctuary, which was grouped with Percé Rock to form a Quebec provincial park in 1985.

▼ **Fathom Five National Marine Park, Ontario** The rock pillars of Flowerpot Island are a major tourist attraction in this park, just off the Bruce Peninsula.

▲ **Gaspé Peninsula** The massive limestone block of Percé Rock is the most recognizable feature of Quebec's east coast.

▶ **Point Pelee National Park** A floating boardwalk winds along the edge of a marsh at the southernmost point in Ontario.

Romantic Quebec City

Yves Tessier
PHOTOGRAPHER

A CITY OF HISTORY, CULTURE AND EMOTION, WHOSE SECULAR WALLS AND PICTURESQUE SCENES TRANSCEND TIME, QUEBEC PROVIDES A WEALTH OF INSPIRATION FOR PHOTOGRAPHERS TO EXPLORE.

Founded in 1608 by Samuel de Champlain, Quebec is a spectacular city with a commanding view of the mighty St. Lawrence River. Quebec's scenic vistas provoke an atmosphere of romance as you explore the narrow streets of Old Quebec's historic district, a UNESCO World Heritage Site. I am especially drawn to the European ambiance of Place-Royale in Quebec's Basse-Ville (Lower Town). Champlain's first dwelling was built here, where today you'll find the Notre-Dame-des-Victoires church. Bordered by stone houses dating back to the 17th and 18th centuries, the neighbourhood has the look and feel of a small village in France. The Quartier Petit Champlain, the oldest commercial district in North America, is alive with warm and inviting cafés and upscale boutiques. I enjoy the intimacy of these streets as I blend in with visitors and soak up their wonder of the sights.

Old Quebec's Haute-Ville (Upper Town) has its own breathtaking vantage points. Encompassing the Citadel and the imposing Château Frontenac, the city's profile is a wonder to behold. In the distance, you can discern the outline of the Laurentian Mountains and l'Ile d'Orléans, where the St. Lawrence River opens wide. Watching activities unfold along picturesque rue du Trésor, where artists display their wares outdoors in summer and winter alike, is a favourite pastime of mine.

Upper Town also offers magnificent light displays in the evening, with changing colours reflecting playfully off building arcades, attic windows, archways and bell towers. In season, the Jeanne-d'Arc floral gardens near the Grande-Allée add their own explosion of colour to this joyous mix. And in the port, the bassin Louise affords exceptional views of Old Quebec's northern flank, with the Pavillon du Séminaire standing as a city landmark.

With its many cafés, terraces and bars, the Grande-Allée is a destination of choice for both visitors and locals. Les Fêtes de la Nouvelle-France (Festival of New France) brings friendly fun to the forefront with giant puppets, festooned in dazzling colours, walking alongside smiling historical figures in period costume. As a photographer, I sometimes feel out of place, snapping photos of a bygone era with my digital camera. But the sheer joie de vivre surrounding me never fails to transport me back in time.

▲ **Ice Palace** The annual Carnaval de Quebec is celebrated every February and has become the world's largest winter festival.

◀ **Château Frontenac** Sunrise awakes the hotel and historic Place-Royale.

▲▲ **Porte Saint-Jean** New France comes to life in Old Quebec. The Porte Saint-Jean is one of the two large gates through Quebec's historic wall.

▲ **Old Quebec** A beautiful, colourful street in the city's historic heart. From the quietly romantic to the overtly festive, Quebec is alive with activities all year round.

Cottage Country

◀ **Lake Massawippi, Quebec** Colourful fall foliage glows above lake-front buildings in Quebec's Eastern Townships.

▼ **Toronto** Mallards flying in the early evening sun.

▼▼ **Oxtongue Lake, Ontario** Youngsters sit at the water's edge near Algonquin Provincial Park's west gate.

▲ **Muskoka, Ontario** A row of lakeside Muskoka chairs sit idle between Labour Day and Thanksgiving.

▶ **Lake Memphrémagog, Quebec** The autumn sun sets over the Saint-Benoît-du-Lac Abbey.

▼ **Red Lake, Ontario** Two pairs of Ojibwa-style wooden snowshoes near a northern Ontario trapline at dawn.

▲▲ **Manitoulin Island** Scenic Gore Bay glows with the hues of early autumn.

▲ **Toronto** A raccoon peeks out of a broken window in Kensington Village.

▶ **Ways Mills, Quebec** A field of sunflowers catches the evening light in the Eastern Townships.

"I know a man whose school could never teach him patriotism, but who acquired that virtue when he felt in his bones the vastness of his land, and the greatness of those who founded it."

—Pierre Elliot Trudeau

▲ **Îles de la Madeleine, Quebec** A brightly-painted fisherman's house is almost a perfect match for the bright sky.

THE ATLANTIC

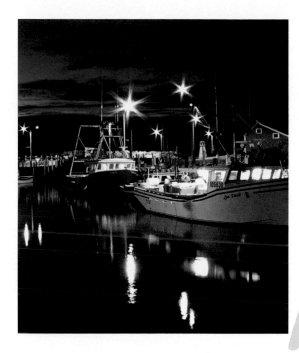

◄ **Cap Egmont, Prince Edward Island** Erosion carves P.E.I.'s sandstone cliffs into unique formations and stains the surrounding ocean with the island's characteristic red earth.

Secluded, Historic and Unspoiled Atlantic Canada

Gail MacMillan

I've always been a proud Canadian delighted to live in the Atlantic provinces. I can stand on jagged cliffs or sandy beaches, the briny ocean with all its changing moods and moments coming right to my feet. Rolling farms and unspoiled forests provide a backdrop where each change of season brings its own delights.

March offers the sweet treat of maple syrup. May welcomes the unique culinary experience of "a feed of fiddleheads." August brings a crop of blueberries. All summer long, the specialties of the fresh boiled lobster and cedar plank salmon grace the tables of church suppers.

By mid-September, nature takes on a breathtaking panorama of colour as trees metamorphose to gold, orange and red. January sees all four provinces gently enveloped in a shimmering blanket of white.

Atlantic Canada has towns and cities but is still largely a region of villages and rural reaches where good Samaritanism remains a way of life, where pitching in to help a neighbour comes as naturally as borrowing an egg or lending a cup of sugar. No one is ever too busy to help a friend or welcome a visitor. A relaxed way of life reminiscent of previous eras makes the Atlantic provinces a place its sons and daughters are proud to call home.

From the picturesque villages on the hillsides of Newfoundland and Labrador's coves to the red, potato-rich soil of Prince Edward Island to Nova Scotia's foggy, sea-bound coasts to New Brunswick's unspoiled verdant forests, Atlantic Canada is rooted in my heart and is the place I'll forever rejoice to call home.

Rediscovering New Brunswick

André Gallant
PHOTOGRAPHER

AS A TRAVEL PHOTOGRAPHER, I'VE SEEN BEAUTIFUL PLACES IN THE WORLD: THE ROLLING HILLS OF TUSCANY OR THE TREASURES OF THE YUCATÁN PENINSULA. BUT WHEN I WAS HIRED TO PHOTOGRAPH NEW BRUNSWICK FOR AN AD CAMPAIGN, I GAINED A NEW APPRECIATION FOR THE BEAUTY AND SOUL OF MY NATIVE PROVINCE.

▲ **Saint John** The largest in New Brunswick and Canada's oldest incorporated city. Under the blue-collar exterior of mills and refineries lies a town with beautiful old homes and people full of heart. Visit the Saint John City Market, the Reversing Falls and the Festival by the Sea.

▲◀ **Fundy National Park** The Point Wolfe covered bridge in Albert County.

◀ **St. Martins** Fifty kilometres north from Saint John is a beautiful village with a quaint harbour and two covered bridges. You can witness the effect of the changing tides, especially obvious when the fishing boats in the harbour lean sideways in the mud at low tide. Six hours later, they're floating secured to the dock. The pebbled beaches, the caves carved by the ocean, and the lobster and seafood chowder all make a trip to St. Martins worthwhile.

I started along the northern shore, stopping to photograph in Campbellton and Bathurst on my way to Caraquet, on the southern coast of Chaleur Bay. Then to Le Village Acadien, a recreation of a village that interprets Acadian life between 1770 and 1949. These were my own ancestors, and it was fascinating to learn about their culture and lifestyle.

The Caraquet Festival, an annual celebration of Acadian culture, began the next day with the blessing of the fleet, one of the most colourful displays in New Brunswick. After the local fishing vessels were blessed, the parade of decorated boats sailed out to sea. I lingered with les Acadiens for a couple of days, then slowly headed towards Miscou Island, at the northeastern tip of the province, and then south along the coast through picturesque towns with names like Shippagan and Tracadie. I organized a sunrise shoot in

Kouchibouguac National Park, located on the coast between Miramichi and Moncton. The name, of Mi'kmaq origin, means "river of long tides," and exquisite beaches, marshes and tidal rivers make this a haven for naturalists.

Heading south, I stopped in Bouctouche to photograph Le Pays de la Sagouine, a recreation of a 1950s fishing village built on L'Ile-aux-Puces—Flea Island—that serves as a backdrop for the learning experience of a lifetime. From Bouctouche, I made my way to Parlee Beach, the most popular beach in New Brunswick—because of its warm water.

Chignecto Bay lies at the northeastern end of the Bay of Fundy. There, you'll find the Hopewell Rocks, where at low tide you can walk on the ocean floor among gigantic "flower pot" rock formations carved by some of the world's highest tides. In early August, hundreds of thousands of shorebirds,

113

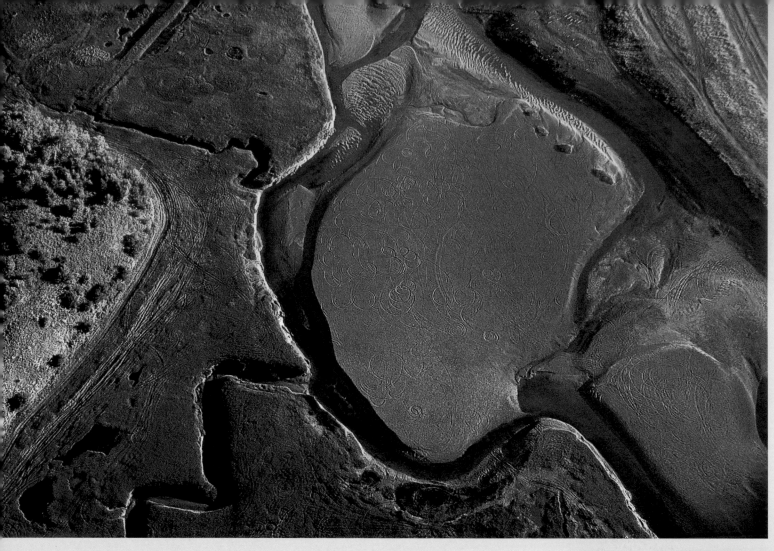

◄ **Bay of Fundy** Bird's-eye view of Martin Head.

▼◄ **Hartland-Somerville** The world's longest covered bridge, which stretches 391 metres across the Saint John River, was originally opened in 1901 as an uncovered bridge. A roof was added in 1922.

▼ **Machias Seal Island** The Atlantic puffin is one of several bird species that finds sanctuary on this Gulf of Maine island.

▲ **Grand Manan** Beached dories and a fishing boat in the morning mist.

especially sandpipers, come to feed on the rich bounty in the mud flats at low tide. When the birds take off, their flight makes for an incredible display that looks like an undulating wave in the sky.

In the southernmost part of the province, where the Bay of Fundy meets the Gulf of Maine, is Grand Manan Island. A one-and-a-half-hour ferry crossing from Blacks Harbour got me to the island, where I stayed photographing beautiful Swallowtail Lighthouse, and Machias Seal Island, with its comical residents, the Atlantic puffins. Then I headed northwest, first to Campobello Island, then to Deer Island. Time seems to stand still on these islands with no traffic and no fast-food chains. Fishing is still the way of life.

St. Andrews by-the-Sea, a tiny coastal village, lies in the southwest of New Brunswick. It's home to the grand Algonquin Hotel, and is a good place to set out whale watching. August is the prime viewing month.

I love to photograph New Brunswick. I'm fortunate to have had so many opportunities to rediscover my province's stunning scenery, simple way of life and friendly people. New Brunswick is a place I'm proud to call home.

▼ **Miscou Island** Fishing is the island's main industry, though residents also do brisk business in peat moss.

Lighthouses

◀ **Cape Breton, Nova Scotia** The lighthouse at Neils Harbour provides a beacon on the island's northeast coast.

◄◄ **Cape Spear, Newfoundland and Labrador** The Cape Spear Lighthouse, near St John's, is the easternmost lightouse in North America.

◄ **Rose Blanche, Newfoundland and Labrador** Built in 1871 from granite obtained from the local quarry, the lighthouse operated between 1873 and the 1940s.

▼ **Charlottetown, Prince Edward Island** The Brighton Beach Range Front Lighthouse underwent major repairs after a storm surge in 2000.

Down through beautiful New Brunswick
and across the P.E.I.
To the rock-bound coasts of Newfoundland,
I'll love them till I die
But if God came here on Earth with us
and asked if he could rest
I'd take him to my Nova Scotia home,
the place that I love best."

—Hank Snow

▲ **Saint John, New Brunswick** Market Square glistens under the glow of streetlights on a rainy evening.

▲ **North Ingonish, Nova Scotia** Waves break over the wharf at MacLeods Point.

◄ **Peggys Cove, Nova Scotia** The spectacular setting has long made this cove a postcard favourite.

▲ **Trinity East, Newfoundland and Labrador** A centuries-old way of life ended when the moratorium on cod fishing was announced in 1992.

► **St. John's, Newfoundland and Labrador** Cabot Tower sits atop Signal Hill, the site where Guglielmo Marconi received the first transatlantic wireless signal in 1901.

Our Ocean Playground

Dale Wilson
PHOTOGRAPHER

Nova Scotia is surrounded by water and renowned for its breathtaking natural scenery, historic sites, timeless fishing villages and vibrant cities. It also has a rich ethnic and cultural heritage that is celebrated throughout the year and across the province.

Raised on a farm, I have a strong sense of being connected to the land of my home province of Nova Scotia. When I was growing up beside the River Hebert, at the northern end of the Bay of Fundy across from Sackville, N.B., my brother and I used to explore along Rector Brook, where centuries of erosion have cut steep banks down ten metres or so to an exposed dry stream bed. Breaking open the layered shale and slate, we would sometimes find fossilized fern leaves dating back some 300 million years.

Little did we know that not far away on either side of the Chignecto Peninsula—our farm was located pretty much in the peninsula's centre—eroding shorelines offered discoveries much grander in scale. At Joggins, on the north shore, the constant, twice-daily scrubbing and scouring of the Fundy tides was exposing the very first reptiles seen on the planet, while on the Minas Basin shoreline to the south, near Parrsboro, people were finding evidence of dinosaurs from some 200 million years ago.

Today, I live with my wife and two children in a village called Eastern Passage, a Halifax suburb that offers a rural environment 30 minutes from downtown. With my camera, I'm still exploring Nova Scotia and all its variety, and the easiest way for me to show it to you is through my pictures.

Nova Scotia contributes about half the 40,000 tonnes of the annual crustacean catch along its 7,500 kilometres of coastline. For years, the lobstermen and fishermen depended on lighthouses to see them home, and the lighthouse pictured at left, at Belliveau Cove on St. Mary's Bay, has been keeping watch over local shipping since 1889. At low tide the boats you see will be lying on their sides in the mud, as all the seawater will have retreated to the Bay of Fundy.

Pockets of Acadian culture flourish throughout Nova Scotia and make a large contribution to the colourful mosaic of the province. Some homes on Isle Madame off the southeast coast of Cape Breton Island, are painted in the Acadian colours: the red, white and blue of France with a gold star (see above, right).

◄ **St. Mary's Bay** Fishing boats moored near the lighthouse at Belliveau Cove.

◄ **Annapolis Royal** A soldier in period costume patrols the ramparts of Fort Anne National Historic Site; this was the scene of numerous 17th- and 18th-century battles fought between France and England for control of the continent.

▼ **Cape Breton** A home painted in Acadian colours on Isle Madame.

▼▼ **Annapolis Valley** Long one of Nova Scotia's main agricultural regions, the Annapolis Valley exports fruit and vegetables worldwide, and has begun producing award-winning wines.

Cape Breton Island

Cape Breton Island has a well-established reputation for fine hospitality, wonderful music and spectacular scenery, once prompting Alexander Graham Bell to write, "I have travelled around the globe. I have seen the Canadian Rockies, the Andes, the Alps and the Highlands of Scotland, but for simple beauty, Cape Breton outrivals them all." The seat of ancient culture and hub of the Celtic music revival, Cape Breton is where Scottish traditions and Gaelic folklore come alive. Bagpipes and fiddles echo through the glens, starting in the rocky shore near the Canso Causeway to the incredible plateaus of Cape Breton Highlands National Park, along the Cabot Trail. This highway, carved into the sides of mountains rising above the Gulf of St. Lawrence and the Atlantic Ocean, offers fabulous vistas. Whales can often be spotted offshore, and bald eagles soar above.

▲ **Halifax** The modern buildings of the downtown core and the centuries-old brick-and-mortar buildings from the days of sail give Halifax a dynamic look.

◀ **Minas Basin** Erosion from the Fundy tides gives Five Islands Provincial Park a dramatic coastline.

Grand Pré National Historic Site is the shrine of the Acadian people, where the tragic and epic story of the great deportation of 1755 is told. Many descendants of those deported eventually found their way back to Acadie, and thousands returned recently on a pilgrimage to celebrate the 400th anniversary of the arrival of French explorer Samuel de Champlain.

And, as they do every summer, thousands of tourists will also visit Peggys Cove, a national icon just southwest of Halifax. With the second largest natural harbour in the world, Halifax continues to be the business epicentre of eastern Canada.

I've always had an interest in history, and as I get older, my interest in Nova Scotia's Aboriginal heritage—a heritage that dates back some 11,000 years—continues to increase. I took a canoe trip, travelling with a group of Boy Scouts to Kejimkujik National Park and National Historic Site, in Nova Scotia's west end. Kejimkujik celebrates the province's Aboriginal heritage by maintaining the land in its natural state, just as it might have appeared when the Mi'kmaq culture first arrived here more than 2,000 years ago.

As the bow of my canoe cut silently through the water, I enjoyed a few moments of quiet solitude amid the tranquility of calling loons and sun-basking turtles, and found myself thinking of the countless times the Mi'kmaq must have taken this very route.

▲ **Mahone Bay** The bay's famous "Three Churches" (St. James Anglican, St. John's Lutheran and Trinity United) glow in the late July sun.

▶ **Lobster boat** Atlantic Canada is the world's largest harvester of Atlantic lobster, and Nova Scotia contributes about half the annual catch.

▶▶ **Digby County** The Balancing Rock stands near Tiverton, on Long Island. Over time, tidal erosion has washed away all the basalt rock that once surrounded this column, leaving it perched precariously to await its inevitable fall.

BENEATH THE BLUE ATLANTIC SKY
WEALTH FROM THE SHELF

"Farewell to Nova Scotia, your sea-bound coast
Let your mountains dark and dreary be.
For when I am far away on the briny ocean tossed,
Will you ever heave a sigh, or a wish for me?"
—*Popular Sea Shanty*

Whether it's fisheries, oil and gas developments, farming, forestry or tourism, all owe their existence to the marvelous diversity of physical features that constitute the unique Atlantic ecozone.

THE CONTINENTAL SHELF AND THE GULF STREAM
The continental shelf spreads 500 kilometres south and east from Newfoundland and Labrador and 200 kilometres southeast of Nova Scotia. Dozens of undersea plateaus, known as banks, lie across the shelf. Water depths on the banks are generally less than 100 metres and create an excellent environment for fish reproduction and growth. Meanwhile, the Gulf Stream brings equatorial waters to the Atlantic provinces before crossing the ocean, resulting in temperate and ice-free waters off Nova Scotia and in the Bay of Fundy.

NORTHWEST ATLANTIC'S "ICEBERG ALLEY"
This marine ecozone stretches from the mouth of Lancaster Sound in the southern Arctic to the Grand Banks, where the frigid south-flowing Labrador Current merges with the Gulf Stream. The current moves icebergs from the Arctic towards Newfoundland and Labrador. "Iceberg Alley" as these waters are called, is not ice-free until July. More than 20 species of whale, notably humpback and bluefin, are found here.

THE BAY OF FUNDY
Every day, some 100 billion tonnes of seawater flows in and out of the Bay of Fundy during one tide cycle—that's more than the combined flow of the world's freshwater rivers. There are two tides every 24 hours. Tidal bores measuring 16.3 metres, higher than a five-story building, have been recorded in Minas Basin. These massive tides' erosive action uncovers fossils, which can be discovered nearly every day on Nova Scotia's Parrsboro Shore.

▲ Blue Rocks, Nova Scotia This tiny fishing community clings to the edge of the Atlantic Ocean, not far from Lunenburg.

▶ Rocky Point, Prince Edward Island Blockhouse Point Lighthouse, near the western end of Charlottetown Harbour, is the second-oldest lighthouse on P.E.I.

◀ Newfoundland and Labrador Fishermen untangle their nets from a large piece of floating ice.

◀◀ Hopewell Rocks Park, New Brunswick The Hopewell Rocks flowerpot formations are the remains of an ancient mountain range. The dramatic rock formations are the products of the Bay of Fundy's amazing tides.

125

WIND, WAVES AND WILD HORSES
SABLE ISLAND—"GRAVEYARD OF THE ATLANTIC"

"It is a world that exists by its own rules, a place without trees, without shade, and without shelter."
—Roberto Dutestco

Sable Island is an uninhabited, 41-kilometre crescent of shifting sand dunes in the Atlantic Ocean some 300 kilometres southeast of Halifax. Named for the French word for sand, "sable," it's home to many species of plants and animals, including about 350 wild horses and half a dozen Environment Canada personnel. Permission to visit the island must be obtained from the Canadian Coast Guard, as the island is protected under the Shipping Act.

WILD, WILD HORSES
The feral horses of Sable Island have long been an inspiration for nature photographers. Today's chestnut, palomino and black stallions are the descendants of horses confiscated from Acadians deported from Nova Scotia to the American colonies. The horses were introduced to the island in 1760 by Boston ship owner, Thomas Hancock. The horses are protected by law and are entirely unmanaged. They roam freely, forage for water and food, and form their own social herd hierarchies—but they have no protection from weather, predators and disease. No human interference of any kind is allowed.

"PERFECT STORM" WEATHER
Legend has it that there have been over 350 shipwrecks off Sable Island since the mid-1500s and over 10,000 people have lost their lives. Sunken ships, the graveyards of the victims, litter the shoals and shallows of the continental shelf seabed surrounding Sable. Strong gales and sea swells continually re-shape this bleak crescent, which is battered by strong winds of up to 130 km/h. The treeless terrain offers little protection for the horses and other wildlife that live on this inhospitable island. Sable is also the foggiest place in all of the Maritimes with an average of 127 days per year with at least one hour of fog. In tandem with the wind and fog, frequent and sudden storms and hurricanes helped secure Sable's reputation as the "Graveyard of the Atlantic."

126

▶ **Sable Diet** For most of the year, there is ample fresh water, plants and grasses to sustain the island's horses.

◀ **Wildlife** The island's herds of wild horses share the land with harbour and grey seals.

▲ **Stormy Weather** The last vessel wrecked on the island was the small yacht *Merrimac*, in 1999.

▶ **From Coast to Coast** The island is a sandbar 41 kilometres long, and no more than 1.5 kilometres wide.

The Wonderful Wilderness of Prince Edward Island

John Sylvester
PHOTOGRAPHER

▶ **Cavendish Beach** Cavendish Beach is blessed with the warm waters of the Gulf Stream.

▼ **Cape Tryon** The north shore's high sandstone cliffs are home to colonies of cormorants.

▼▼ **Cold coast** A harp seal lounges on the shore in eary winter.

WILDERNESS ISN'T THE FIRST THING THAT COMES TO MIND WHEN YOU THINK OF PRINCE EDWARD ISLAND. AFTER ALL, CANADA'S SMALLEST AND MOST DENSELY POPULATED PROVINCE IS BETTER KNOWN FOR ITS SPUDS THAN FOR ITS WILDLIFE. BUT THE ISLAND BOASTS A SURPRISING VARIETY OF NATURAL AREAS.

Prince Edward Island National Park is one of Canada's smallest national parks with an area of just 21½ square kilometres. Best known for beaches that attract thousands of tourists every summer, the park provides diverse habitat for a variety of plants and animals, including the red fox, beaver, bald eagle and shorebirds such as the rare piping plover.

The magnificent Greenwich dunes were added to Prince Edward Island National Park in 1998 and this remarkable area had gained recognition from the United Nations International Biological Program and the World Wildlife Endangered Species Program. Its most significant feature is the rare parabolic dunes, huge crescent-shape sandhills formed by prevailing onshore winds, which cause them to migrate inland up to four metres each year. They leave behind a series of low ridges called counter ridges, or gegenwälle. These are colonized by marram grass, which anchors the sand by its extensive root system and allows other species such as wild rose, bayberry and beech pea to take root. It is the only site in North America where gegenwälle is found.

The dunes migrate slowly, burying nearby forest and exposing previously buried trees—known as a skeletal forest. Aboriginal artifacts dating back over 10,000 years and relics from the Acadian settlers have been discovered.

The Townsend Woodlot, north of Souris, is one of the best old-growth hardwood groves in the province. Walking among its towering sugar maples and beech trees, it's easy to imagine what the island must have looked like centuries ago, before settlers arrived. In spring, the forest floor is sprinkled with wildflowers such pink lady's slipper, P.E.I.'s floral emblem.

The province's wetlands have not changed much since human settlement began. Malpeque Bay, renowned for its oysters, is also an internationally designated wetland. Its shallow waters and salt marshes—a haven for migrating geese and ducks—are protected from the open sea by Hog Island, one of a series of barrier islands that stretch for 40 kilometres along the island's northwest coast.

Bogs are a different wetland. Walking across one is like walking on a giant sponge—rubber boots and good balance are mandatory! P.E.I.'s bogs were formed thousands of years ago when receding glaciers left depressions in the land from which water couldn't drain. Slowly the depressions filled in with vegetation. Sphagnum moss is the predominant plant in this oxygen-deprived and acidic environment. It decays and becomes peat, enabling other hardy plants to take root, including the unusual insect-eating pitcher plant and round-leaf sundew.

My favourite time to explore P.E.I.'s coast is fall, when I photograph wind-inspired sand patterns, and migrating flocks of shorebirds. Powerful autumn storms wash away dunes—in some areas the coast erodes a metre a year. But where land is lost in one area, it's sure to be gained in another, usually on a sandbar or beach. The effects of wind and water ensure the island's constantly changing profile.

▲ **Hog Island** The largest of the barrier islands along P.E.I.'s northwest coast is known for its amazing dune, salt marshes and barren heaths.

◄ **Sea View** Millennia of salty tides have carved these cliffs into whimsical shapes.

▼ **Attack!** A red fox pounces on its prey.

Untamed Newfoundland and Labrador

Greg Locke
PHOTOGRAPHER

THE POWER AND BEAUTY OF THE LAND AND SEA ARE THE BACKDROP FOR THE STORIES OF THE LIVES, STRUGGLES, TRIUMPHS AND DREAMS OF A PEOPLE OF THE SEA.

▶ **CFB Goose Bay** RAF Tornadoes at a NATO training base in Labrador.

▼ **An ice catch** Fishermen retrieving cod traps in early spring.

There's something about a small homogeneous society like Newfoundland and Labrador, with its storied past and purpose, that gives you a sense of belonging to something tangible and rooted. To know your history and culture is to know yourself and to feel a part of something. It gives you a confidence of being and explains why a local will ask, "Where do you belong?" instead of "Where are you from?"

The poet and novelist Michael Crummey has said that the province "may be the most un-Canadian part of Canada."

The irony is that the "New Founde Lande" is the birthplace of Canada's exploration, starting in 1497 with the arrival of the Venetian explorer Giovanni Caboto, or John Cabot, as he was known to his employers, the merchants of Bristol in England's southwest.

And yet it wasn't until 450 years later that the province officially became a part of the country. Newfoundland and Labrador's entry into Confederation on March 31, 1949, brought the story of Canada full circle, completing the coast-to-coast country.

The soul of Newfoundland and Labrador is in the spirit of her people. It was founded a nation of merchants, fishing admirals, sea traders and those who came with them to earn money. English, Irish, Scottish and French, they formed a new Celtic society and culture that mutated and matured separately from their European cousins, evolving to meet the challenges of life in this harsh place. It was cod that drew men to her waters and shores. Cod was gold and meant riches for merchants.

And though it was, in fact, illegal to settle here until the late 1700s, many did, defying England and the laws of the fishing admirals. At some point they just decided to stay and not return to England. They took on the challenge of not only surviving on these unforgiving shores but thriving and living in coexistence with the place, taking food, fuel and shelter from the land and the sea without having to or trying to tame her wildness.

Newfoundland and Labrador's physical beauty remains untamed and uncultivated. The savage, foreboding seascapes, cliffs of stone and barren sub-Arctic tundra are breathtaking and awe-inspiring, a landscape to be feared and respected by even those who were born into it.

▶ **St. John's** New Gower Street shines as New Year's Eve fireworks explode over the harbour.

◀ **Hibernia Oil Field** The Hibernia oil platform is the largest in the world, and sits about 315 kilometres east ot the Avalon Peninsula.

▼ **St. John's** Master boat builder Jerome Canning puts the finishing touches on a dory.

Flora & Fauna

▶ **Ingonish, Nova Scotia** The number of great-horned owls in Nova Scotia has dropped in recent decades.

▶ **Prince Edward Island National Park** The seaside playground is home to sand dunes, barrier islands and wetlands.

▼ **Orwell Cove, Prince Edward Island** The vibrant colours of late June at a hillside farm southwest of Montague in central P.E.I.

▶ **Nashwaak Valley, New Brunswick** A doe treds carefully past hay bales on a farm just north of Fredericton.

▶▶ **Perth, New Brunswick** Fiddleheads appear in spring, often growing in moist conditions.

▼ **Red Rocks, Nova Scotia** Bay of Fundy tides provide an abundant supply of food for gulls near Cape Chignecto Provincial Park.

NEWFOUNDLAND AND LABRADOR
LAND OF PHYSICAL BEAUTY AND RICH CULTURAL HERITAGE

"Pity the poor creatures in warmer countries where the seasons never change. Where summer is eternal and they never know the pain of waiting and the joy at last when summer comes."

—Ray Guy

Last to join Confederation in 1949, Newfoundland, Canada's easternmost province, officially changed its name to "Newfoundland and Labrador" in December 2001.

GROS MORNE NATIONAL PARK
Located on the west coast of the island of Newfoundland and designated a UNESCO World Heritage site in 1987, Gros Morne has a cornucopia of natural wonders, from mountains and waterfalls to a glacier-fed freshwater fjord and sandy beaches.

GANDER
The city of Gander dates only to the 1950s, but its world famous airport has been in service since the 1930s. Gander provided safe haven for thousands of passengers and crew on September 11, 2001, when North American airspace was closed following the attacks on New York and Washington. Dozens of transatlantic flights diverted to the international airport.

▲ **Point of Bay** Colourful handmade snowshoes in a small community on the north shore fjords northwest of Gander.

134

TERRA NOVA NATIONAL PARK

Located on the east coast of the island of Newfoundland, the park takes its name from the Latin for "Newfoundland." Terra Nova is a land where the raging north Atlantic and the inland boreal forest live side by side. Designated Newfoundland's first national park in 1957, it is popular with kayakers, anglers and hikers.

THE ROYAL NEWFOUNDLAND CONSTABULARY

Though the Royal Newfoundland Constabulary's (RNC) current form dates back to 1844, the organization's beginnings can be traced back to 1729, which makes it the first civil police force in North America. The RNC's true distinction, however, is that it was the last police force on the continent to be armed. The force began carrying weapons as part of normal operations only at the end of the 20th century.

◄ **Cape Spear** North America's easternmost point is a national historic site and features the province's oldest surviving lighthouse.

▼ **St. John's** Shrimp and crab boats enter St. John's Harbour at the end of the day.

◄ **Nain** Located on the shore of Unity Bay, the Inuit village is protected from the raging Atlantic by numerous small islands.

▲ **Orwell Corner Historic Village, Prince Edward Island** A girl dressed as Anne of Green Gables takes a stroll down a country lane.

"Isn't it splendid to think of all the things there are to find out about? It just makes me feel glad to be alive— it's such an interesting world."

▲ **Cavendish, Prince Edward Island** The Green Gables farmhouse that served as inspiration for the house in Lucy Maud Montgomery's most famous novel.

▲ **Gaspereaux, Prince Edward Island** Fishermen set their nets at the end of a long day.

▶ **Liverpool, Nova Scotia** A die-hard surfer braves the icy winds of January, looking for that one perfect wave.

▼ **Fogo Island, Newfoundland and Labrador** St. Andrew's Anglican Church dwarfs the surrounding buildings of the picturesque town of Fogo in the early morning mist.

THE NORTH

"LAND ISN'T A HERITAGE FROM
OUR PARENTS—IT'S A LOAN
WE OWE TO OUR CHILDREN."
—FIRST NATIONS PROVERB

Dreaming of Northern Canada

Mike Beedell

Prime Minister Mackenzie King once said "Canada has too much geography" and I could not disagree with him more. In our north country we are blessed with millions of square kilometres of seacoast, national parks and wild lands that protect crucial habitat, water quality and remote indigenous communities.

For 33 years I have spent much of my time as a photographer and guide. I continue to explore and document the rugged and challenging geography of our north and the unique people who live towards the end of the earth.

The most western Canadian extremity of the 60th parallel is my favourite ski touring places in the world—Kluane National Park, Yukon and the extraordinary massif of Mount Logan, Canada's highest peak. From the summit at 5,959 metres, I have looked out breathlessly with my mountaineer teammates—in awe of the spectacular highways of ice flowing into Canada and Alaska.

Another type of highway, the Dempster, which starts in the Yukon just north of Dawson, is my favourite road in the world. It leads you all the way to Tuktoyaktuk and the Arctic Ocean in the Northwest Territories.

Now head farther north to Grise Fiord, Nunavut, on Ellesmere Island. This is North America's most northerly community with fewer than 150 hardy souls.

From Grise Fiord it is only another 1,544 kilometres to the north pole, and on your way you must visit Quttinirpaaq National Park. You can see herds of Arctic hare romping on the plains, white wolves chasing down wooly muskoxen or an Arctic tern that has flown 16,000 kilometres to raise it's young.

I encourage all Canadians to experience one of these magical places—you will feel more Canadian for having done so.

◄ **Yukon** A rotary rail snowplow clears the White Pass & Yukon Route Railway's line.

Nunavut is Our Land

Mike Beedell
PHOTOGRAPHER

NUNAVUT OFFERS ENDLESS QUANTITIES OF POETIC LIGHT, BUT FROM APRIL TO JULY IT IS PARTICULARLY ENTHRALLING. FOR FOUR MONTHS OF THE YEAR, NIGHT NEVER COMES, AND THE LAND IS BATHED IN DAYLIGHT 24 HOURS A DAY.

▲ **Northwest Territories** Made from seal or caribou skins, mukluks allow hunters to silently pursue their prey.

▶ **Ellesmere Island** An Arctic wolf on the prowl on Nunavut's Ellesmere Island.

▶▶ **Nunavut** An Inuk child keeps warm with animal furs.

145

N.W.T. North of 60

Robert Postma
PHOTOGRAPHER

I HAVE FALLEN IN LOVE WITH THE NORTH. THE TRANQUILITY OF A SUNSET, AWE-INSPIRING WATERFALLS, THE HAUNTING DISPLAY OF THE NORTHERN LIGHTS... THESE THINGS CALL TO ME, AND AWAKEN MY SENSES.

Morning dawns clear and crisp in Fort Simpson. Waves caress the banks of the mighty Mackenzie River as our float plane rocks gently in the current. We're headed for Virginia Falls and Glacier Lake, both within the boundaries of Nahanni National Park Reserve, a UNESCO World Heritage Site, near the Yukon border.

We head west over a land punctuated with lakes, trees and muskeg as the Mackenzie Mountains become visible ahead. The lakes give way to the daunting mountains of the park. As we fly over Ram Plateau, we watch Dall sheep grazing on the mountainside grasses. They take little notice as we soar overhead towards the canyon where the South Nahanni River has gouged its course into the bedrock.

Virginia Falls drop an impressive 90 metres, making it one of Canada's highest waterfalls. It is a wonder to behold from the air, but much better experienced up close. You can feel the ground tremble from the force of the South Nahanni flowing over the precipice.

Glacier Lake, surrounded by the dramatic granite cliffs of the Cirque of the Un-climbables, shines an enticing blue. The stories about it are true: the water is numbingly cold, and the cliffs soaring around us beckon to mountain climbers looking for a challenge.

Before moving to the Northwest Territories, I always wondered what life was like for the people living there. The North is sparsely populated, with some 43,000 people located in a relatively small number of communities separated by great distance and a rugged landscape. Yellowknife, the capital, is a bustling city of about 18,000. One of the busiest float-plane bases in the world, it offers all of the amenities of the South, but on a smaller scale. There's dining out, live theatre, golf and shopping—with a distinctly northern flair.

Since moving to Fort Smith, just north of the Alberta border, I've spent many hours listening to the stories of Dene and Inuit elders, whose tales weave a colourful and dynamic tapestry of their history with the land. Their accounts of tending trap lines, following the caribou herds, and foraging for food, are testaments to their fortitude. There are those who still live the traditional lifestyle. Riding in a komatik being pulled by dogs is one of the cleanest, purest forms of travel.

The last stop is the Thelon Game Sanctuary. Straddling the Northwest Territories-Nunavut border, it is the largest wildlife sanctuary on the continent. Here, the tundra comes alive with rich, vibrant colour, making it a paradise for hikers, nature watchers and canoeists—as well as photographers.

◀◀ **Muskeg** Viewed from the air, the land takes on the colours of a painter's palette.

◀ **Yukon-Northwest Territories border** The landscape and epic sky stretch as far as the eye can see.

▲ **Fort Simpson** The aurora borealis dances above the site of the Pope's 1987 visit to the Northwest Territories.

◀◀ **Virginia Falls** The South Nahanni River cascades almost twice the vertical drop of Niagara Falls.

◀ **Moose** The North is home to some of the country's largest fauna.

147

LIFE IN THE GREAT WHITE NORTH
A BEAUTIFUL AND VAST SPACE FILLED WITH WONDERS

▲ **Iqaluit** With fewer than 7,000 inhabitants, Nunavut's largest community has the smallest population of any provincial or territorial capital in Canada.

▲ **Fairbanks, Alaska** The Yukon Quest sees dogsled teams set out from the course's start in Fairbanks to race 1,600 kilometres to the finish in Whitehorse.

"The land is the source of our collective identity—it shapes our culture and our language. The land is our life."

—James Arvaluk

NORTHWEST TERRITORIES (N.W.T.)

A mixture of rocky taiga and frozen tundra, the N.W.T. is home to 40,000 Dene, Inuvialuit and Métis. Within this vast territory, only the Mackenzie Delta and Great Slave Lake areas are accessible by road. In some places, the permafrost is 500 metres deep.

THE YUKON

The Yukon gets its name from the Gwich'in name *Yu-kan-ah*, which means "Great River." At 3,185 kilometres long, the Yukon River is one of the longest in North America. The territory's main industries are mining and tourism, with kayaking, hunting and fishing attracting outdoors enthusiasts from around the world.

NUNAVUT

Canada's third territory borders five provinces, N.W.T. and Greenland. Eighty-five per cent of Nunavut's 30,000 inhabitants are Inuit.

ALERT

Alert is the northernmost permanently-inhabited place. It's named for H.M.S. *Alert*, a British sloop captained by Sir George Strong Nares during his exploration of the area.

"EXPLORE CANADA'S ARCTIC"

North America's only non rectangular vehicle licence plates belong to the Northwest Territories. The blue and white plates are in the shape of a polar bear with the slogan above.

◄ **Yellowknife** The legislative assembly of the Northwest Territories was designed with circular consensus-style chambers within.

▼ **Dawson City** The picturesque city on the Yukon River still shows its Gold Rush roots.

My Yukon Home

Richard Hartmier
PHOTOGRAPHER

ON THE FEW OCCASIONS THAT I'VE TRAVELLED OUTSIDE THE TERRITORY, I COULD MEASURE MY ADDICTION TO HOME BY THE INTENSITY OF MY DESIRE TO RETURN. SOME MIGHT CALL IT MY LOVE AFFAIR WITH THE YUKON, BUT PIERRE BERTON SUMMED IT UP BEST WHEN HE DESCRIBED US AS "PRISONERS OF THE NORTH."

The Yukon Territory is 483,450 square kilometres of mountain ranges and valleys, separated from the Pacific Ocean by the Alaskan panhandle. Straddling the Arctic Circle, the Yukon lies north of the 60th parallel and contains 8,052 square kilometres of rivers, lakes and watershed. Western coastal mountains, including Canada's highest peak, Mount Logan (5,959 metres) in the St. Elias mountain range, and the Selwyn, Richardson and Pelly mountains on the east, rim this vast northern land. Climate conditions that kept part of the Yukon ice-free during the last ice age allowed animals and the ancestors of North American aboriginal nations to migrate across the Beringia land bridge from Asia.

The Yukon made its mark on the world map with the discovery of gold in 1896 and the subsequent Klondike Gold Rush. It was one of a series of stampedes for gold that began in California and ended on the sandy beaches of Nome, Alaska. The notoriety of the gold rush was assured, in part, because it coincided with a worldwide depression, seizing the attention of masses who were galvanized into travelling north. This period in the Yukon's rich history was well-documented in photographs and motion pictures—Thomas Edison even had a film crew here. Suddenly, the Yukon captured the imagination of the continent, and the world.

Here, the subarctic climate allows average temperatures to rise above 10ºC for just four months of the year. Winter's long, dark nights and cold, clear days—combined with the mild summer days and nights—create a magical setting for photography.

FOCUS ON GOLD RUSH

Klondike Dream

The August 1896 discovery of gold along the Yukon's Rabbit Creek sparked off one of the last great gold rushes. During the year or so of the Klondike Gold Rush, the population in the area rose to the tens of thousands. To stave off unrest and famine, the North West Mounted Police closed the border to would-be prospectors who weren't packing at least a year's supply of food or who refused to leave their guns at the border.

But Klondike Fever also resulted in other mineral discoveries, including base metals in Manitoba and radium near Great Bear Lake. Silver and gold discoveries were also happening all over the Canadian Shield, as prospector's wended their way north-westward in search of riches. In fact, there is still some gold mining happening in the Klondike area today.

▲ **Whitehorse** A colourfully attired Tlingit dancer on a cliff overlooking the Yukon River.

◄ **Yukon River** Adventurers whitewater kayaking on the Yukon River near Whitehorse.

◄◄ **Emerald Lake** South of Whitehorse, the water's distinctive colour comes from sunlight reflecting off the clay lake bed.

151

The Yukon is abundant with wildlife in its natural pristine environment: moose, caribou, deer, mountain goats, timber wolves and bear. Waterfowl wow the photographer each spring as geese, ducks, swans and shorebirds migrate to their northern nesting grounds. Salmon, Arctic grayling, northern pike and trout swim in our lakes and rivers. Our farmers' markets are summer showcases for the oversized vegetables grown beneath the midnight sun. Autumn cranberries, high-mountain blueberries the size of marbles, wild raspberries, strawberries and currants keep both the grizzlies and the humans well-fed. Clean air and crystal clear water, wide open spaces and gorgeous geography—not to mention the opportunity to experience golden silence just minutes outside of Whitehorse, the territory's capital—are all reasons why I'm proud to call the Yukon home.

Kluane National Park and Reserve, a UNESCO World Heritage Site, is home to a vast array of wildlife and plant life, dramatic icefields and Canada's highest mountains. Although Whitehorse is home to 25,000 of the Yukon's 33,000 inhabitants, many smaller communities such as historic Carcross, Haines Junction, Carmacks and Watson Lake dot the Alaska Highway.

What brings people here? Mining—for sand, gravel, silver and gold—is still important. Governments—territorial, aboriginal and federal—are other areas of employment. It may seem hard to believe, but although the Yukon is one of the most geographically isolated places in Canada, it's also one of the most technologically connected. But change is afoot here in the North just as it is everywhere else.

Tourists and newcomers arrive and pay more attention to the values of wilderness and open spaces. Outdoor winter sports, such as snowmobiling, ice fishing, snowboarding and some of the best backcountry telemarking, are very popular. And in summer, rivers and lakes are a paradise for fishing and provide endless places to explore by kayak or canoe, while old mining roads are maintained and serve to offer world-class hiking trails and mountain bike paths. The Yukon is, indeed, a great place to be.

▲▲ **Near Dawson City** A trio of hikers stand in awe of the beauty before them.

▲ **Yukon River** Midnight sun turns the Yukon River to gold near Dawson City.

▲ **Kluane** Mount Logan looms behind a charter plane used in summer to transport visitors to wilderness cabins.

◄ **Teslin** Totem poles stand guard outside the Teslin Tlingit Heritage Centre.

"Unconsciously, Canadians feel that any people can live where the climate is gentle. It takes a special people to prosper where nature makes it so hard."

—Robert MacNeil

▶ Iqaluit, Nunavut
A racer and dogs rest before the start of 320-km race to Kimmirut and back.

► **Baffin Island, Nunavut** A lone traveller walks through pools of meltwater in Admiralty Inlet.

▲ **Yukon** A family of Stone sheep browses by the side of a road.

► **Fort Simpson** The sun sets over the Mackenzie River as it winds its way past a docked float plane and on towards the Arctic Ocean.

"I believe the world needs more Canada."

—Bono

OUR CONTRIBUTORS

The editors wish to express their sincere gratitude to all the contributors to this book, for without their generosity and support, *Our Canada, Picture Perfect*, would not have been possible.

Cover Sylvia Prins, Beamsville, Ont.
Back Cover
Jennifer Thorn, Burnaby, B.C.
Sandra Kidder, Aldergrove, B.C.
Nancy Hamilton, Meaford, Ont.
Chris Pawluk, Carstairs, Alta.

2 Michel Lamarche, Longueuil, Que.
5 Kevin Dunn, Penticton, B.C.
6 James Hutchison, Burnstown, Ont.
6 Darren Metcalfe, Corunna, Ont.
6 Harry Ogloff, Salmon Arm, B.C.
7 Victoria Phillips, Inuvik, N.W.T.
7 Wayne Sullivan, Sudbury, Ont.
8 Anne Burkard, Rosalind, Alta.
8 Elaine Hall, Victoria, B.C.
8 Daniel Zantingh, Emsdale, Ont.
9 Martin (Marty) Courchesne, Penticton, B.C.
9 Lou Ricci, Norval, Ont.
9 Kevin Ward, Allardville, N.B.

British Columbia

12 Garth Lenz, Victoria, B.C.
14 Sheri Filice, Rosedale, B.C.
15 Debra Cannon, Salmon Arm, B.C.
16–20 Al Harvey, Vancouver, B.C.
21 Gail Hourigan, Kelowna, B.C.
21 Wayne Lutz, Powell River, B.C.
21 Janice Rand, Bridgewater, N.S.
21 Jeff Sotropa, Cranbrook, B.C.
22 Barb Hansen, Victoria, B.C.
22 Al Harvey, Vancouver, B.C.
23 Robin Clay, Toronto, Ont.
24 Jim Brompton, Saskatoon, Sask.
24 Al Harvey, Vancouver, B.C.
24 Dave Rolston, Prince Rupert, B.C.
24 Tom Skinner, Vernon, B.C.
24 Karen Thompson, Kelowna, B.C.
25 Brent Embree, 108 Mile Ranch, B.C.
25 Fuzzy Harrison, Crofton, B.C.
25 Kristen Lunman, Westbank, B.C.
26–27 Emma Levez Larocque, Powell River, B.C.

28 Richard Evans, Surrey, B.C.
29 Jenny Eng, Coquitlam, B.C.
30 Sandra Kidder, Aldergrove, B.C.
31 Clare Moster, Selkirk, Man.
32–35 Gunter Marx, Burnaby, B.C.
36 Al Harvey, Vancouver, B.C.
36 Helen Szuuts, Clandeboye, Man.
36 Karen Thompson, Kelowna, B.C.
36 Donald and Witt Whittaker, Calgary, Alta.
37 Dawn Lawson, Port Coquitlam, B.C.
37 Wayne Lutz, Powell River, B.C.
37 John Marriott, Canmore, Alta.
38–39 Dave Rothwell, Kelowna, B.C.
40–41 Gordon Baron and Cindy Phillips, Dawsons Landing, B.C.
42 Gillian Hoyer, New Westminster, B.C.
42 Susan LePage, Vancouver, B.C.
42 Linda McCormack, Dieppe, N.B.
44 Peggy Linton, Cobourg, Ont.
45 Neil Jorgenson, Errington, B.C.
45 Mark Joyce, Nelson, B.C.
45 Anthony Lemphers, Sherwood Park, Alta.
46–47 David Lambroughton, Armstrong, B.C.
48 Kyle Girgan, Nanaimo, B.C.
48 Jordan Lester, Thunder Bay, Ont.
49 Gordon Baron and Cindy Phillips, Dawsons Landing, B.C.
49 Douglas Halladay, Rossland, B.C.

The West

50 Mike Grandmaison, Winnipeg, Man.
52 John Marriott, Canmore, Alta.
53 Robin and Arlene Karpan, Saskatoon, Sask.
54–57 Todd Korol, Calgary, Alta.
58–59 Todd Korol, Calgary, Alta.
58 Marie Nylund, Sundre, Alta.
59 Daryl Benson, Edmonton, Alta.
59 Deryk Bodington, Calgary, Alta.
60–64 John Perret, Saskatoon, Sask.
65 David Reede, Winnipeg, Man.
66 Garnet Boutette, St. Albert, Alta.
67 Victor Epp, Medicine Hat, Alta.
68 Gary Foucault, Calgary, Alta.
68 Allan Harrison, Edson, Alta.

68 Pat Lovatt, Carroll, Man.
68 Kathy Wolos, St. Francois Xavier, Man.
69 Trish Olsen, Neilburg, Sask.
69 John Perret, Saskatoon, Sask.
69 Angela Sterling, Calgary, Alta.
69 Paula Ritchie, Winnipeg, Man.
69 Sandra Schindel, Red Deer, Alta.
70–73 David Reede, Winnipeg, Man.
74 Les Dunford, Dapp, Alta.
74 Robin and Arlene Karpan, Saskatoon, Sask.
74 Don Mickle, Canmore, Alta.
74 John Perret, Saskatoon, Sask.
74–75 Clarence Norris, Saskatoon, Sask.
75 Todd Korol, Calgary, Alta.
75 Kevin Friesen, Steinbach, Man.
75 Wayne Shiels, Saskatoon, Sask.
76 Howe Sim, Acton, Ont.
77 Robin and Arlene Karpan, Saskatoon, Sask.

Central Canada

78 Jean-François Leblanc, Montreal, Que.
81 Yves Tessier, Quebec, Que.
82–85 Mike Grandmaison, Winnipeg, Man.
84 John Hartig, Vineland, Ont.
87 Michael Winters, Toronto, Ont.
88–91 Frank H. Scheme, Ottawa, Ont.
92 Dominic Cantin, Quebec, Que.
92 Glenn Holtzhauer, Cambridge, Ont.
92 Michel Lamarche, Longueuil, Que.
92 Tom McCabe, Guelph, Ont.
93 Beth Ann Hay, Chipman, N.B.
94 Gilles Delisle, Montreal, Que.
95 Jean-François Leblanc, Montreal, Que.
97 Gilles Delisle, Montreal, Que.
97 Glen Tanaka, North York, Ont.
98 Nick Aloe, Toronto, Ont.
98 Jean-François Leblanc, Montreal, Que.
98 Peter Morgan, Halifax, N.S.
99 Jean-François Leblanc, Montreal, Que.
100 Gilles Delisle, Montreal, Que.
100 Ron Erwin, Scarborough, Ont.
100 Mike Grandmaison, Winnipeg, Man.
101 Cara Shody, Kitchener, Ont.
102–103 Yves Tessier, Quebec, Que.
104 Jocelyn Boutin, Sherbrooke, Que.
104 Paul Chalmers, LaSalle, Ont.
104 Derek Wojtczak, Timmins, Ont.
105 Jocelyn Boutin, Sherbrooke, Que.
105 Kaaren Dannenman, Red Lake, Ont.
105 Ron Erwin, Scarborough, Ont.
105 Daniel Zantingh, Emsdale, Ont.
106 Jocelyn Boutin, Sherbrooke, Que.
106 Paul Cuthbert, London, Ont.

106 Ron Erwin, Scarborough, Ont.
107 Gilles Delisle, Montreal, Que.

The Atlantic

108 Wayne Barrett and Anne MacKay, Cornwall, P.E.I.
110 Wayne Barrett and Anne MacKay, Cornwall, P.E.I.
111 Bill Davenport, Kentville, N.S.
112–115 André Gallant, Saint John, N.B.
116 Greg Ferens, Ingonish, N.S.
117 Patrick Allen, Charlottetown, P.E.I.
117 Helen Kaulbach, Kelowna, B.C.
117 Scott Young, Botwood, N.L.
118 Greg Ferens, Ingonish, N.S.
119 Dave Harron, Estevan, Sask.
119 Greg Locke, St. John's, N.L.
120–123 Dale Wilson, Eastern Passage, N.S.
124 Greg Locke, St. John's, N.L.
125 Kathleen Thompson, Halifax, N.S.
126 Damian Lidgard, Halifax, N.S.
126 David Nichols, Fall River, N.S.
127 Len Wagg, Wellington, N.S.
128–129 John Sylvester, Charlottetown, P.E.I.
130–131 Greg Locke, St. John's, N.L.
132 Greg Ferens, Ingonish, N.S.
133 Wayne Barrett and Anne MacKay, Cornwall, P.E.I.
133 Matthew Traer, Fredericton, N.B.
133 Len Wagg, Wellington, N.S.
134 Greg Locke, St. John's, N.L.
134 Gloria Young, Botwood, N.L.
136 Wayne Barrett and Anne MacKay, Cornwall, P.E.I.
137 Wayne Barrett and Anne MacKay, Cornwall, P.E.I.
137 Wendy Booth, Kanata, Ont.
137 Corinne Burton Mars, Liverpool, N.S

The North

138 Randy Burns, Calgary, Alta.
140 Cathie Archbould, Whitehorse, Y.T.
141 Catherine Olsen, Edmonton, Alta.
142-144 Mike Beedell, Chelsea, Que.
144 Ben Avern, Yellowknife, N.W.T.
145 Mike Beedell, Chelsea, Que.
146-147 Robert Postma, Marsh Lake, Y.T.
148 Kimberley Watkins, Whitehorse, Y.T.
149-153 Richard Hartmier, Whitehorse, Y.T.
154 Lyn Nye, Truro, N.S.
154 Jeff Parsons, Whitehorse, Y.T.
155 Mike Beedell, Chelsea, Que.
155 Margita Davey, Lower Nicola, B.C.
155 Robert Postma, Marsh Lake, Y.T.

PHOTO CREDITS

Credits are left to right, top to bottom

Cover Sylvia Prins; **Back Cover** Jennifer Thorn, Sandra Kidder, Nancy Hamilton, Chris Pawluck.
Front Inside Cover Barrett & Mackay;
2 Michel Lamarche; 5 Kevin Dunn; 6 Harry Ogloff; James Hutchison; Darren Metcalfe; 7 Wayne Sullivan; Victoria Phillips; 8 Elaine Hall; Anne Burkard; Daniel Zantingh; 9 Lou Ricci; Kevin Ward; Martin (Marty) Courchesne; 12–13 Garth Lenz; 14 Sheri Filice; 15 Debra Cannon; 16–20 Al Harvey; 21 Gail Hourigan; Janice Rand; Jeff Sotropa; Wayne Lutz; 22 Al Harvey; Barb Hansen; 22–23 Robin Clay; 24 Dave Rolston (ghosted background); Jim Brompton; Karen Thompson; Tom Skinner (center); Al Harvey; 25 Fuzzy Harrison; Brent Embree; Kristen Lunman; 26–27 Emma Levez Larocque; 28 Richard Evans; 29 Photography West; Jenny Eng; 30 Sandra Kidder; 30–31 Clare Moster; 32–35 Gunter Marx; 36 Karen Thompson; Helen Szuuts; Donald Whittaker (ghosted background); Al Harvey; 37 Wayne Lutz; Dawn Lawson; John Marriott; 38–39 Dave Rothwell; 40–41 Gordon Baron & Cindy Phillips; 42 Philip Date/Fotolia.com (Background); Gillian Hoyer; Susan Le Page; Linda McCormack; Maxx Images; 43 courtesy Capilano Suspension Bridge; 44 Peggy Linton; 45 Anthony Lemphers; Mark Joyce; Neil Jorgenson; 46–47 David Lambroughton; 48 Damir Frkovic/Masterfile (left); Kyle Girgan; Jordan Lester; 49 Gordon Baron & Cindy Phillips; Douglas Halladay; 50–51 Mike Grandmaison; 52 John Marriott; 53 Robin & Arlene Karpan; 54–57 Todd Korol; 58 Marie Nylund; Todd Korol; 59 Todd Korol; Daryl Benson; Todd Korol; Deryk Bodington; 60–64 John Perret; 65 David Reede; Rubens Abboud/Getstock; 66 Garnette Boutette; 67 Victor Epp; 68 Kathy Wolos; Gary Foucault (ghosted background); Allan Harrison; Pat Lovatt; 69 Sandra Schindel; Angela Sterling (right center); John Perrett (left center); Paula Ritchie; Trish Olsen; 70–73 David Reede; 74 Clarence Norris (ghosted background); John Perret; Robin & Arlene Karpan; Les Dunford; Don Mickle; 75 Clarence Norris; Kevin Friesen; Todd Korol; Wayne Shiels/Lone Pine Photo; 76 Howe Sim; 76–77 Robin & Arlene Karpan; 78–79 Jean-François LeBlanc; 80 Ontario Tourism; 81 Yves Tessier;

82–83 Mike Grandmaison; 85 John Hartig; 84–85 Mike Grandmaison (5); 86 Benjamin Rondel/Firstlight; 87 Ken Straighton/Firstlight; Paul Irish/GetStock; Michael Winters; 88–91 Frank Scheme; 92 Glenn Holtzhauer (ghosted background); Michael Lamarche; Tom McCabe; Dominic Cantin; 93 Beth Ann Hay; 94 Gilles Delisle; 95 Jean-François Leblanc; F. Hudec/Firstlight; Jean-François Leblanc; 96 Don Johnston/Ivy Images; 97 Gilles Delisle; Hans Blohm/Masterfile; Glen Tanaka; 98 Peter Morgan; Nick Alo; 98–99 Jean-François Leblanc; 99 Wikwemikongheritage.org; Jean-François Leblanc; 100 Gilles Delisle; Mike Grandmaison (ghosted background); Ron Erwin; 101 IStock; Cara Shody; 102–103 Yves Tessier; 104 Jocelyn Boutin; Ron Erwin (ghosted oar); Derek Wojtczak; Paul Chalmers; 105 Daniel Zantingh; Karen Dannemann; Jocelyn Boutin; 106 Ron Erwin; Paul Cuthbert; Jocelyn Boutin; 107 Gilles Delisle; 108–110 Wayne Barrett; 111 Bill Davenport; 112–115 André Gallant; 116 Greg Ferens; 117 Helen Kaulbach; Scott Young; Patrick Allen; 118 Wayne Barrett; Greg Ferens; 119 Dave Harron; Greg Locke; Barrett & Mackay; 120–121 Dale Wilson; 122 Barrett & Mackay; 122–123 Dale Wilson; 124 Dept. Tourism and Parks N.B. (left); Greg Locke; 125 Kathleen Thompson; Barrett & Mackay; 126 Damian Lidgard (2); David Nichols/Prisma Productions; 127 Len Wagg; 128–129 John Sylvester; 130–131 Greg Locke; 132 Kim D. French/Fotolia.com(background); Greg Farens; Barrett & Mackay (2); 133 Matthew Traer; Barrett & Mackay; Len Wagg; 134 Gloria Young; Barrett & Mackay; 135 Newfoundland and Labrador Tourism; Greg Locke; 136 Barrett & Mackay (2); 137 Barrett & Mackay; Wendy Booth (left); Corinee Burton Marsh; 138–139 Randy Burns; 140 Cathie Archbould; 141 Catherine Olsen; 142–143 Mike Beedell; 144 Mike Beedell (2); Ben Avern; 145 Mike Beedell; 146–147 Robert Postma; 148 Joanna B. Pinneo, Aurora Photos/Getstock; Kimberley Watkins; 149 Government NWT; Richard Hartmier; 150–153 Richard Hartmier; 154 Jeff Parsons; Lyn Nye 155 Mike Beedell; Margita Davey; Robert Postma; Rommel/Masterfile;
Back Inside Cover Barrett & Mackay.

MUSIC LYRICS CREDITS

30 CANADIAN RAILROAD TRILOGY: Words and Music by GORDON LIGHTFOOT, © 1967 (Renewed) EARLY MORNING MUSIC. Used by Permission of ALFRED MUSIC PUBLISHING CO., INC. All Rights Reserved.
38 Excerpt From: "The Snowmobile Song." Written By Tom. C Connors. Copyright 1970 Crown-Vetch Music, S.O.C.A.N. All Rights Reserved.
96 Excerpt From: "Sudbury Saturday Night." Written By Tom. C Connors. Copyright 1970 Crown-Vetch Music, S.O.C.A.N. All Rights Reserved.
118 MY NOVA SCOTIA HOME: Words and Music by HANK SNOW © 1959 (Renewed) HANK SNOW MUSIC and UNICHAPPELL MUSIC, INC. All Rights Administered by UNICHAPPELL MUSIC, INC. All Rights Reserved. Used by Permission of ALFRED PUBLISHING CO., INC.